ITSM LIBRARY

*it*SMF International
The IT Service Management Forum

Implementing ISO/IEC 20000 Certification

The Roadmap

VHP

About the ITSM Library

The publications in the ITSM Library cover best practice in IT management and are published on behalf of itSMF International.

The IT Service Management Forum (itSMF) is the association for practitioners and organizations who practice IT Service Management. itSMF's goal is to promote innovation and support of IT management. Suppliers and customers are equally represented within the itSMF. The Forum's main focus is exchange of peer knowledge and experience. Our authors are global experts.

The following publications are, or soon will be, available.

Introduction, Foundations and Practitioners books
- Foundations of IT Service Management based on ITIL® (covers V2, Arabic, Chinese, German, English, French, Italian, Japanese, Korean, Dutch, Brazilian Portuguese, Russian, Danish and Spanish).
- Foundations of IT Service Management based on ITIL® V3 (English, Dutch; versions in German, French, Italian, Japanese, Spanish due Spring 2008)
- IT Service Management - An Introduction (covers V3, English)
- IT Services Procurement based on ISPL - An Introduction (Dutch)
- Project Management based on PRINCE2™ 2005 Edition (Dutch, English, German)
- Release & Control for IT Service Management, based on ITIL® - A Practitioner Guide (English)
- ISO/IEC 20000 - An Introduction (English)

IT Service Management - best practices
- IT Service Management - best practices, part 1 (Dutch)
- IT Service Management - best practices, part 2 (Dutch)
- IT Service Management - best practices, part 3 (Dutch)
- IT Service Management - best practices, part 4 (Dutch)
- IT Service Management - Global Best Practices, part 1 (English)

Topics & Management instruments
- IT Service Management - Global Best Practices, part 1 (English)
- Metrics for IT Service Management (English)
- Six Sigma for IT Management (English)
- The RfP for IT Outsourcing - A Management Guide (Dutch)
- Service Agreements - A Management Guide (English)
- Frameworks for IT Management (English, German, Japanese)
- IT Governance based on COBIT® - A Management Guide (English, German, Japanese)

Pocket Guides
- IT Service Management - A summary based on ITIL® (covers V2, Dutch)
- IT Service Management Based on ITIL® V3 - A Pocket Guide (English, Dutch; versions in German, French, Italian, Japanese, Spanish due Spring 2008)
- ISO/IEC 20000 - A Pocket Guide (English, German, Japanese, Italian, Spanish)
- IT Services Procurement based on ISPL - A Pocket Guide (English)
- IT Service CMM - A Pocket Guide (English)
- Six Sigma for IT Management - A Pocket Guide (English)
- Frameworks for IT Management - A Pocket Guide (English, Dutch)

Miscellaneous
- IT Service Management from Hell!! (covers V2, English)
- IT Service Management from Hell. Based on Not-ITIL (covers V3, English)

For any further enquiries about ITSM Library, please visit www.itsmfbooks.com or www.vanharen.net.

Implementing ISO/IEC 20000 Certification:
The Roadmap

*it*SMF **International**
The IT Service Management Forum

Van Haren
PUBLISHING

Colophon

Title:	Implementing ISO/IEC 20000 Certification: The Roadmap
Author:	David Clifford - FISM[1]
Editors:	Jan van Bon (Chief Editor) Selma Polter (Editor) Tieneke Verheijen (Editor)
Copy editor:	Jayne Wilkinson
Publisher:	Van Haren Publishing, Zaltbommel, www.vanharen.net
Design and Layout:	CO2 Premedia bv, Amersfoort - NL
ISBN:	978 90 8753 082 2
Edition:	First edition, first impression, February 2008

Permission to reproduce extracts from BS ISO/IEC 20000-1:2005 & BS ISO/IEC 20000-2:2005 is granted by BSI. British Standards can be obtained in PDF format from the BSI online shop: http://www.bsi-global.com/en/Shop/ or by contacting BSI Customer Services for hardcopies: Tel: +44 (0)20 8996 9001,
Email: cservices@bsi-global.com

ISO (the International Organization for Standardization) and IEC (the International Electrotechnical Commission) form the specialized system for worldwide standardization. National bodies that are members of ISO or IEC participate in the development of International Standards through technical committees established by the respective organization, to deal with particular fields of technical activity. ISO and IEC technical committees collaborate in fields of mutual interest. Other international organizations, governmental and non-governmental, also take part in the work, in liaison with ISO and IEC. In the field of information technology, ISO and IEC have established a joint technical committee, ISO/IEC JTC 1.
International Standards are drafted in accordance with the rules given in the ISO/IEC Directives, Part 2.
The main task of the joint technical committee is to prepare International Standards. Draft International Standards adopted by the joint technical committee are circulated to national bodies for voting. Publication of an International Standard requires approval by at least 75 % of the national bodies casting a vote.

ISO/IEC 20000 is the official name of the standard. In the field, the standard is referred to as '**ISO 20000**'. For practical reasons, the shorter and more practical title for the standard has been used.

For any further enquiries about Van Haren Publishing, please send an email to:
info@vanharen.net

---

1 FISM - Fellow of the Institute of IT Service Management - ISM

Foreword

By John Stewart, Director of Procurement Policy and Standards in the UK Government's Office of Government Commerce (OGC), who was responsible, with the late Pete Skinner, for the ITIL concept. John led the early development of ITIL and once again has lead responsibility for it in OGC.

"Business increasingly depends on technology-enabled services". These are the first words in section 1.1 of this book. They were also the words we used twenty years ago to make the case to develop ITIL. Little did we know at the time that there would be personal computers on nearly every desk, with the potential for networked access to computers anywhere else in the world. We only had the vaguest idea of how dependent organizations would become on IT, and how "stuck" we would become if the system or the network were down.

We didn't have the terminology to express it then but the idea of *service quality management* permeated our early thinking. That was exactly the medicine, packaged as ITIL, that organizations were needing to tame the technology on which their success and smooth running would increasingly depend.

And as project developers we took our own medicine: we were among the very first organizations in the UK government to obtain ISO 9001 certification for the way we ran ITIL and related developments.

We knew it wasn't just UK government that was becoming dependent on IT, so we took steps to make ITIL available to the widest possible audience internationally. We talked from the earliest days about the idea of an international standard complementing ITIL and based on it. How gratifying that the community has made it happen.

ITIL's success is a result of the hard work of many people. I would like to signal OGC's encouragement to the many organizations around the world, offering products and services based on ITIL. They provide the channels through which the wider community can reap the benefits of businesses effectively deploying IT.

On that endeavour may you all have success.

John Stewart

Acknowledgements and project layout

ISO/IEC 20000, the international standard for IT Service Management, attracts much of attention in the field. Many organizations and individuals are looking into the opportunities offered by the standard, and get together to discuss this. The Dutch ISO/IEC 20000 Early Adopter Group, a working group that emerged as a result of this growing interest, was used as an initial review board for the structure of this book.

The idea to develop this roadmap book for an ISO/IEC 20000 certification project initially emerged from the editorial team of itSMF International's ITSM Library. The fact that this standard was so closely related to the core readership of the ITSM Library, combined with the lack of practical guidance, made it very clear that a roadmap publication would serve the itSMF community very well.

The basic structure for this publication was the result of a study by Selma Polter and Jan van Bon, of the ITSM Library team, and was derived from existing quality management literature, editorial principles used in the ITSM Library, and interviews in the field. This basic structure was then reviewed by the ISO/IEC 20000 Early Adopter Group and a number of individual experts, which resulted in a further improvement of the book's design.

Based on this first design, Jan van Bon and Tieneke Verheijen invited a number of ISO/IEC 200000 certified organizations to describe their practical certification experience in a case document, along the logic of the book's design. They tried to reach as many certified organizations as they could find, and found six organizations who were happy to participate. We wish to thank all organizations for their contributions and willingness to share their experiences. We also wish to thank a number of people who have generously provided time and information for the different case descriptions. They are, starting from the first case study in this book:
- Jan Boogers (Quality Manager EDS-ITO, the Netherlands), who was interviewed by Tieneke Verheijen
- Johan van Middelkoop (Quality Manager EDS-ITO, the Netherlands), who was interviewed by Tieneke Verheijen
- Masumi Taira (ITSM Manager Fujitsu FIP Corporation, Japan), who authored the Fujitsu FIP Corporation case study
- Kumi Yasui (Japanese Quality Association, Japan), who put us in touch with Masumi Taira from Fujitsu FIP Corporation
- Jaap van Staalduine (CEO ING Service Centre Budapest, Hungary), who co-authored the ING Service Centre Budapest case study
- Gábor Patay (CIO ING Service Centre Budapest, Hungary), who co-authored the ING Service Centre Budapest case study
- Manisha Champaneri (IT Service Management and ISO 20000 Consultant, Marval, United Kingdom), who authored the Marval case study
- Paul Breslin (ICT Sector Leader DNV Industry BeNeLux, United Kingdom), who put us in touch with Manisha Champaneri from Marval

- Foo Nian Chou, (Chief IMS, Infrastructure Management and Solutions, NCS Pte Ltd, Singapore), who co-authored the NCS case study
- Chew Hwee Hong, (Senior Manager PQM, Process & Quality Management, NCS Pte Ltd, Singapore), who co-authored the NCS case study
- Christiane Chung Ah Pong, (Lead Consultant PQM, Process & Quality Management, NCS Pte Ltd, Singapore), who co-authored and coordinated the NCS case study
- Tsuneo Noda - (ISO 20000 training course director, IP innovations inc., Japan), who co-authored the Nippon Securities Technology case study
- Masahiko Tsumura (ISO 20000 Consultant, IP innovations inc., Japan), who co-authored the Nippon Securities Technology case study
- Ryoji Nakamura (Executive Officer, Operation Division, Nippon Securities Technology Co., Ltd., Japan), who was interviewed by Tsuneo Noda and Masahiko Tsumura
- Shingo Yagi (Manager, Operation Division, Nippon Securities Technology Co., Ltd., Japan), who was interviewed by Tsuneo Noda and Masahiko Tsumura
- Takehisa Makino (Engineer, Operation Division, Nippon Securities Technology Co., Ltd., Japan), who was interviewed by Tsuneo Noda and Masahiko Tsumura

During the development of these case documents, several improvements were made to the initial book design. This ensured that 'the roadmap' was valid in practice, and was illustrated by the structure of several case descriptions.

Having finalized the case descriptions, the next step was the development of a generic roadmap for other organizations facing a certification project. This required very practical insight into such a certification project, and a significant helicopter view. We were very happy to find **David Clifford** (FISM), Head of Consulting Practice at PRO-ATTIVO, willing to spend his energy on this project. David had the required practical experience, with many years' experience as a worldwide consultant, lecturer and conference speaker on the topic of ISO/IEC 20000, its forerunners, related frameworks and methods. He is the President Elect of the Institute of IT Service Management. And very important: David was willing to share his knowledge with the rest of the market. With the support of his family: Denise, Emily and Francesca, he was able to spend a significant number of hours on the development of this publication.

A very important role was also played by the Review Team. This team was composed of a wide variety of professionals from various countries:
- Pierre Bernard - Pink Elephant Inc - Canada
- André Bogert - Infor - The Netherlands
- Koen Brand - Steenbok Adviesgroep - The Netherlands
- Hartger Brasjen - Ideas to Interconnect - The Netherlands
- Bernd Broksch - Siemens AG - Germany
- Rob van der Burg - Microsoft - The Netherlands
- Matthew Burrows - BSMimpact.com - United Kingdom
- Christiane Chung Ah Pong - NCS Pte Ltd - Singapore
- Edwin Eichelsheim - Quint Wellington Redwood - The Netherlands
- Rosario Fondacaro - Quint Wellington Redwood - Italy
- Simone Fuchs - SAP - Germany

- Marcus Giese - TÜV SÜD Management Service GmbH - Germany
- Andreas Gräf - Hewlett-Packard - Germany
- Alex Hernandez - Plexent - USA
- Kevin Holland - NHS England - United Kingdom
- Matiss Horodishtiano - Amdocs - Israel
- Wim Hoving - BHVB - The Netherlands
- Brian Johnson - CA - USA
- David Jones (FISM) - Plan-Net Plc - United Kingdom
- Henk Keijzer - KEMA Quality - The Netherlands
- Larry Killingsworth - Pultorak & Associates, Ltd - USA
- Maggie Kneller (FISM) - United Kingdom
- Elixender Lamprea León - Sicelca IT Systems - Venezuela
- Steve Mann (FISM) - SM2 - itSMF Belgium
- Luis F Martínez Sánchez - Gestió i Govern de les TIC (G2TIC) - Spain
- Reiko Morita - Ability InterBusiness Solutions, Inc. - Japan
- Tatiana Orlova - EC-leasing - Russia
- Joel A Pereira (CISM) - The Centre For IT Service Management Pte. Ltd. - Singapore
- Selma Polter - Independent - The Netherlands
- Silvia Prickel - United Airlines - USA
- Roger Purdie - Q-Venture - Australia
- Claudio Restaino - BITIL.COM - Italy
- Mart Rovers - InterProm USA - USA
- Leo van Selm - Vaseom b.v. - The Netherlands
- Cheryl E. Simpson - Independent - USA
- Masumi Taira - Fujitsu FP - Japan
- Madeleine Townsend - Foster-Melliar - South Africa
- Ray Tricker - Herne European Consultancy Ltd - United Kingdom
- Tony Verlaan - GetronicsPinkRoccade - The Netherlands
- Flip van de Waerdt - HP - The Netherlands
- Stuart Wright (MISM) - PRO-ATTIVO - United Kingdom

The members of the Review Team delivered a large number of improvement issues, which ultimately made this book into what it was meant to be: a very practical roadmap for your ISO/IEC 20000 certification project. All of this work wouldn't have been possible without the extremely dedicated and professional contribution of **Tieneke Verheijen**, the managing editor, who made sure that another top quality publication could be added to the ITSM Library.

Being a very young standard, we expect that further improvements of this ISO/IEC 20000 Roadmap will be possible. We therefore invite all readers to comment on this book, and provide us with any issues that would further enhance its value. Comments can be sent to the chief editor, at j.van.bon@inform-it.org.

Jan van Bon
Managing Editor ITSM Library

x

Contents

Part II: ISO 20000 Certification case studies   93

Case 1: Electronic Data Systems IT Outsourcing   95

Case 2: Fujitsu FIP Corporation 115

Case 3: ING Service Centre Budapest (SCB) 137

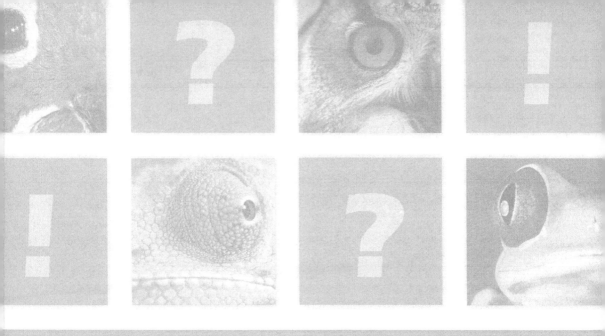

PART I:
GENERAL GUIDELINES ON ISO 20000 IMPLEMENTATION AND CERTIFICATION

Chapter 1

Introduction to ISO 20000

1.1 Why is this subject relevant?

Business increasingly depends on technology-enabled services. Business, as well as IT success, depends more than ever on how well it can deliver against the expectations of an increasingly demanding client base. Well-publicized corporate governance scandals and new regulatory requirements, such as the US Sarbanes-Oxley Act, have led businesses to insist that the IT sector should adopt a *service quality management* (SQM) culture.

ISO/IEC 20000 (abbreviated to ISO 20000 in this book, as explained previously) is an international standard, specifically aiming to establish such service quality management systems in IT organizations. It is increasingly being used as buying criteria in IT outsourcing decisions. ISO 20000 certification is becoming a differentiator, providing competitive advantage for both external, commercially-focused, service providers and internal service providers, who are wishing to demonstrate their capability.

> ISO 20000 is based on demonstrating capability. The service provider can therefore only be either conformant (able to show tangible evidence to confirm that the requirement is being satisfied) to the capability requirements, or non-conformant to the requirements. This is different to maturity, where a service provider is normally assessed against best practice and rated based on five levels.

As Section 1.3.3 explains, with the introduction of the ISO 20000 standard, an IT service provider can, for the first time in history, obtain an independent qualification level that recognizes Service Management capability. Certifying IT staff in ITIL® is a first step, which many IT organizations have taken; the next step is to move up from individual certifications, to an organizational certification, ISO 20000.

The standard promotes the adoption of an integrated process approach for the management of IT services. The standard is quite demanding in what it requires service providers to do, as it addresses a wide array of processes (see Figure 1.1). Most readers of this publication will be familiar with ITIL® version 2 and the Service Support and Service Delivery publications. ISO 20000 documents requirements for the processes covered by these publications, and introduces other management processes which are not addressed by them. Section 1.3.6 provides details of the overarching management processes.

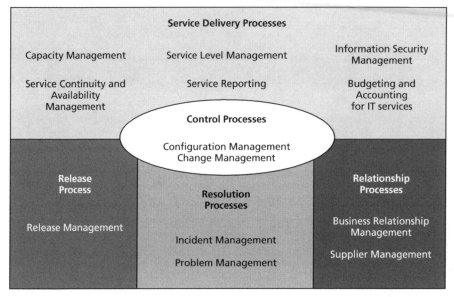

Figure 1.1   IT Service Management (ITSM) according to DISC PD0005 and ISO 20000

ISO 20000 sets out to provide the basic requirements for good and professional practice and quality. The standard does not address organization-specific requirements; for example, legislation of particular interest to an IT service provider, who is providing services in a specific industry, such as financial and banking.

The ISO 9000 family[4] is a generic standard for quality management systems. For an organization that has already been certified against ISO 9001:2000, has implemented all ITIL® service delivery and service support processes, and may be working on adapting the ITIL® version 3 lifecycle approach, certification to ISO 20000 will be easier to achieve. This is because ISO 20000 builds ITSM-specific requirements onto the generic requirements of ISO 9001.

This implementation guide contains practical advice on ISO 20000 certification. It is intended to guide the reader through the requirements and details of the standard, the scoping, the project approach, the certification procedure and the management of the certification process. The first part is a step-by-step description of the ISO 20000 implementation. The second part contains six case studies from ISO 20000 certified organizations. They have shared their experiences, based on a detailed logging structure, including fixed questions following the certification track. This consistent format helps to ensure that all relevant information has been included in these case

---

4   See Section 7.5 for more explanation on how ISO 9000 is composed.

studies. In the first part of this guide, reference to these case studies will be made, to illustrate the information given with practical examples.

This is an implementation guide and, as such, takes a high level approach to process theory and guidelines. For further detail, please refer to the ITSM Library publication *ISO/IEC 20000 - an Introduction*, which is to be published in 2008.

1.2   What is ISO 20000's history?

The International Organization for Standardization published the ISO 20000 standard on 15 December 2005. On this date it was promoted from the British Standard 15000 (BS 15000) to an international standard. BS 15000 described a management system based on the approach used for ISO 9000, but with a specific focus on the management controls required for effective Service Management aligned with ITIL® version 2. The move to ISO 20000 recognized the international nature of IT Service Management (ITSM), by ensuring that the language used in the standard was consistent with other ISO standards. Work continues to bring the language in line with other standards.

BS 15000 was initially introduced in November 2000 by the British Standard Institution (BSI). This British Standard introduced requirements for an ITSM quality management system, in addition to requirements for the quality of the separate ITSM processes. In the early years, itSMF UK received numerous requests from companies wishing to become certified to the standard; this prompted them to introduce a worldwide certification scheme. Global interest continued to grow, and this resulted in the recognized need for an international standard.

BS 15000 originated from DISC PD 0005, A Code of Practice for IT Service Management. DISC PD 0005 was defined by BSI, working with a group of British experts at the end of the 1990s. The standard was designed to bridge the gaps which had not been addressed by ITIL®. The ITIL® books lacked guidance on the design of IT Service Management processes. DISC PD 0005 offered clear guidance on requirements and recommendations.

ITIL® was a starting point which was adjusted and augmented with additional processes, in order to clarify the relationship between them. Figure 1.1 shows the service delivery, service support and security management processes from ITIL® version 2 in a somewhat new grouping. Furthermore, relationship processes and a service reporting process - now included in ITIL® version 3 - have been added[5]. The DISC PD 0005 model was not changed when it evolved to BS 15000 and to ISO 20000.

1.2.1   What is ISO 20000's current context?

As ISO 20000 partly has its roots in ISO 9000, it should be noted that the current version of the ISO 9000 standard was published in the year 2000 (ISO 9001:2000, which is usually abbreviated to 'ISO 9001'). The former 1994 version of ISO 9000 had the reputation of being

---

5 These ITIL-books had not been published at that time and DISC PD0005 was ahead with, for example, acknowledging incident- and release management as separate processes. The names of the processes continuity management and financial management for IT services at the ITIL updates in 2000 and 2001 have also been inspired by DISC PD0005.

'paper intensive', as it led to many documented procedures, but little improvement in the quality services provided by many businesses.

With ISO 9001:2000 this has changed. ISO 9001 has a focus on performance, on continual improvement and customer satisfaction. The extent of documentation can be reduced from the requirements of the previous edition of the standard, depending on the organization, the complexity of its processes and the competence levels of the employees. As the documentation guidelines on the ISO website (www.ISO.org) state, ISO 9001:2000 requires a documented quality management system, and not a system of documents[6].

In May 2007, ITIL® version 3 was published, presenting an umbrella lifecycle model grouping all ITIL® processes into the categories Service Strategy, Service Design, Service Transition, Service Operation and Continual Service Improvement. The concept of continual improvement, based on Deming's PDCA cycle[7], was adopted from ITIL® version 2 into ISO 20000, and given an important position. As a matter of simplification, the service lifecycle phases of ITIL version 3 can be mapped on to the phases of Deming's PDCA cycle. The Service Strategy and Service Design phases can be mapped to the Plan phase, and the Service Transition and Service Operation phases can be mapped to the Do phase. Continual Service Improvement (CSI) embodies the Check and Act phase, while monitoring and reporting on process performance (see Figure 1.2). Of course, each lifecycle phase should also be continually improving itself.

Although ISO 20000 is not formally related to ITIL®, and there is no control defined or implied between the two, it was clear that it was strongly aligned to the ITIL® version 2 books. This means that the changes in content, scope and terminology in ITIL® version 3 are not yet reflected in ISO 20000. However, aligning the new version of ITIL® to ISO 20000 was one of the many briefs given to the authors of ITIL® version 3. Although there are still some differences between the standard and ITIL®, they have never been more aligned.

As an example, ISO 20000 treats service requests as incidents, in the same way that ITIL® version 2 did, while ITIL® version 3 formally separates this into incident management and request fulfillment. It is to be expected that the next update of ISO 20000 will reflect the contents of ITIL® version 3 'best practice'. This may take some time, since ISO standards go through a rigorous change process to ensure that a quality product is produced. It is not recommended, however, that readers wait for the next version of the standard, as this will be some time away from issue, and significant benefits can be achieved with the current version. The case studies in Part 2 show how companies can benefit from the current version, and indeed, much can be gained from this version. Moreover, an auditor would be likely to accept version 3 practice as supporting the progression towards ISO 20000, as the standard recognizes that a service provider may be using one of any number of the many different Service Management frameworks in existence.

---

6 ISO (2001). *Introduction and Support Package. Guidance on the Documentation Requirements of iso 9001:2000*. Document: ISO/TC 176/SC 2/N525R. Available through: www.iso.org/iso/en/iso9000-14000/explore/transition/2000rev7.html

7 Edwards Deming has been inspired by Walter Shewhart, one of his teachers already advocating a 'learning and improvement cycle'. The P-D-C-A cycle of Edwards Deming is also known as the PDSA-cycle, which stands for 'Plan-Do -Study-Act'. In this case, the results are studied instead of checked.

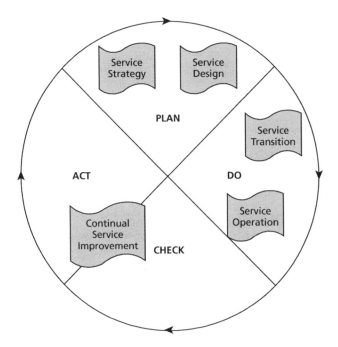

Figure 1.2   Mapping of the ITIL® lifecycle versus Deming's PDCA cycle

1.3   What is ISO 20000?

1.3.1   Targets/goals

ISO 20000 has four primary goals that need to be demonstrated throughout the IT Service Management system; these are:

1. **Customer-Focused** - Throughout the lifecycle of IT Service Management consideration of the customer needs will need to shine through, examples are provided later in this book.
2. **Integrated Processes** - Processes do not work in isolation, and there are clear links between common processes, with information flowing through the management system in a controlled way.
3. **End-to-End Service Management** - An emphasis on managing the supply chain, ensures alignment to the customer commitments that have been made by the service provider.
4. **Continual Service Improvement** - Improvement is applied consistently throughout the management system.

1.3.2   Specification

The ISO 20000 standard is composed of two parts, under the general title Information Technology - Service Management:

• **Part 1: Specification**: Published as ISO/IEC 20000-1: 2005. This is the formal specification of the standard.

- **Part 2: Code of practice**: Published as ISO/IEC 20000-2: 2005. This describes best practices in more detail, and provides guidance and recommendations for the Service Management processes within the scope of the formal standard.

In general, Part 1 of the standard contains a list of mandatory controls, 'shalls' that IT service providers must comply with, in order to become certified. Part 2 contains a list of guidelines and suggestions that 'should' be addressed by IT service providers wishing to become certified.

The list of objectives and controls that ISO 20000-1 provides is not intended to be exhaustive. An organization may need additional objectives and controls to meet its particular business needs, and may find them in supporting frameworks such as ITIL®. ISO 20000-1 states that "the nature of the business relationship between the IT service provider and business will determine how the requirements in ISO 20000-1 are implemented in order to meet the overall objective."

As a process standard, ISO 20000 follows the process approach of ISO 9001:2000 and focuses on continual improvement. As for requirements for management review and internal audit, ISO 20000 draws heavily from ISO 9001. All eight quality management principles of ISO 9000 are found within ISO 20000:
1. customer focus
2. leadership
3. involvement of people
4. process approach
5. systematic approach to management
6. continual improvement
7. factual approach to decision-making
8. mutually beneficial supplier relationships

ISO 9000 describes only general processes, for organization management, for the management of resources, for the realization of the product or service and for measurement, analysis and improvement. It is the international standard for quality management systems. A management system describes the practices that an organization uses to manage its business. A quality management system defines the way in which an organization manages the quality of its products and services.

Table 1.1 summarizes all processes of ISO 9000, ISO 20000 and ITIL® version 2 and 3. Processes in one row of the table are very alike and overlap. ISO 9000 clearly leaves a gap as far as the product realization processes are concerned. This gap is being bridged by the ITIL® Service Management processes and the ISO 20000 requirements (see Figure 1.3).

1.3.3 Accreditation and certification
By collecting the core information of the ITIL® Service Management processes in an international formalized standard, BSI, and now ISO, have the ability to certify IT service providers against compliancy to a sub-set of these best practices. Until BS 15000 was created, the formal certification was focused on individuals (ITIL® Foundation, ITIL® Practitioner and ITIL® Service Manager), rather than on organizations. ISO 20000 certification now provides a certification option that is independent from any other framework.

As has been indicated, the contents of ITIL® can easily be derived from the standard. With ISO 20000, an IT service provider can obtain an international organization-focused certificate for IT Service Management. Service providers can be audited for conformity with ISO 20000 and - if the audit is positive - they can be awarded the certificate by Registered Certification Bodies (RCBs). Certification bodies get their accreditation using ISO/IEC 17021:2006. The itSMF UK also recognizes this accreditation for their independent scheme.

Although service providers can claim their compliance with the specifications of the ISO 20000 standard, a formal audit and certification will carry significantly more weight. This certification already is a default requirement in many contractual agreements, especially in larger outsourcing deals.

IT service providers who want to become certified against the ISO 20000 standard can contact one of the Registered Certification Bodies (RCBs) anywhere in the world, and apply for certification.

Certification bodies are assessed and approved (accredited) by an accreditation organization in any country of their choice, in accordance with ISO/IEC 17021:2006. These accreditation organizations are appointed by governments, to be the sole organization in a country that can accredit certification bodies. The accreditation organization will screen the certification body thoroughly for independency and competence. The itSMF UK, in the UK, but operating internationally, will accept certification body applications only when they originate from certification bodies who are already accredited by their relevant national accreditation body. They can then become a Registered Certification Body (RCB) for ISO 20000 for the independent itSMF UK scheme. Note that an RCB cannot provide specific consultancy advice, as there could be a conflict of interest; an audit must be independent, hence the need to separate audit from consultancy services. The lists of accredited RCBs are available from the accreditation bodies and – for the itSMF UK scheme – from the ISO 20000 website: www.isoiec20000certification. com. Please note, it is the intention of the itSMF UK to migrate accreditation to the National Accreditation Bodies over time; this process has already started.

The RCB will audit IT service providers against the requirements of the standard and issue a certificate. The certification is only valid for three years. Therefore, certified IT service providers will be re-audited on a regular basis to confirm their compliance to ISO 20000. This means surveillance audits every six months and re-certification audits every three years.

Certified IT service providers are permitted to use the provided logo, in accordance with specified restrictions and requirements. They may also opt to be listed on a public web page. For the itSMF UK scheme, additional information on the procedure, the RCBs, the certified IT service providers, and the latest news on ISO 20000 certification can be found on the website www. isoiec20000certification.com.

It is common for an organization to have an assessment, to determine whether it is ready for an audit, before initiating an ISO 20000 audit. This could be done by an external party, but there is also a self-assessment option. To this end, BSI published the *IT Service Management Self-assessment Workbook* (published as BIP 0015). This book contains a checklist that complements

ITIL® version 3	ITIL® version 2	ISO 20000	ISO 9000
		Requirements for a management system	**Processes for organization management**
		Management responsibility, documentation requirements, competence, awareness and training.	Strategic planning, establishing policies, setting objectives, providing communication, ensuring availability of resources needed and management reviews (Plan and Do phase PDCA).
			Processes for managing resources
			Provision of resources needed for processes for organization management, realization and measurement.
Continual Service Improvement	Planning to implement Service Management	**Planning and implementing Service Management**	
		Plan Service Management (Plan)	
		Implement Service Management and provide the services (Do)	
CSI Improvement Process		Monitoring, measuring and reviewing (Check)	
		Continual improvement (Act)	
Service Strategy		**Planning and implementing new or changed services**	**Planning of product realization**
Service Portfolio Management			
Service Design, Service Operation	The business perspective series	**Relationship processes**	**Customer-related processes**
	(+ v1 Customer liaison)	Business relationship management	
Supplier management	(v1 Managing facilities + third party relationships)	Supplier management	
Service desk (first overlap)			
	Service management		**Realization processes**
			All processes that provide the intended output of the organization
Service Strategy, Service Design, Continual Service Improvement	Service delivery	**Service delivery processes**	
Service level management	Service level management	Service level management	
Service reporting	Service reporting (not an autonomous process, but part of service level management)	Service reporting	
Service Catalogue Management			
			Processes for measurement, analysis and improvement
			Processes needed to measure and gather data for performance analysis and improvement of effectiveness and efficiency. They include measuring, monitoring and auditing processes, corrective and preventive actions, and are an integral part of the management, resource management and realization processes (Check and Act phase PDCA).

ITIL® version 3	ITIL® version 2	ISO 20000	ISO 9000
Financial Management	Financial management for IT services	Budgeting and accounting for IT services	
IT service continuity management	IT service continuity management	Service continuity and availability management	
Availability management	Availability management		
Capacity management	Capacity management	Capacity management	
Demand management	Demand management (not an autonomous process, but part of capacity management)		
Information security management	Security management	Information security management	
Service Operation	**Service support**	**Resolution processes**	
Incident management	Incident management	Incident management	
Request Fulfillment	Service desk		
Service desk (second overlap)			
Problem management	Problem management	Problem management	
Service Transition, Service Operation		**Control processes**	
Service Asset & Configuration management	Configuration management	Configuration management	
Change management			
Transition Planning and Support (first overlap)	Change management	Change management	
Service Validation and Testing			
Evaluation			
Service desk (third overlap)	Service desk		
Service Transition		**Release process**	
Release and Deployment Management	Release management	Release management	
Transition Planning and Support (second overlap)			
Out of ISO 20000 scope:	**Out of ISO 20000 scope:**		
Access management	ICT infrastructure management		
Event management	Applications management		
IT Operations			
Knowledge Management			
Monitoring and Control			

Table 1.1 Processes in ITIL® version 2 and 3, ISO 20000 and ISO 9000

the standard. It has been designed to assist organizations to assess the extent to which their IT services conform to the specified requirements. It is recommended that properly qualified staff execute the assessment, as the questions are subjectively based.

As far as personal certification is concerned, the standard is quite succinct on the requirements that staff providing the services should meet. The introduction of Part 1 says:

> It is assumed that the execution of the provisions of this part of ISO 20000 is entrusted to appropriately qualified and competent people.

Currently, itSMF UK, ISEB and EXIN are developing exams for individuals to become proficient in the practices of ISO 20000, including consulting and auditing around the standard. The previously mentioned ITSM Library publication *ISO/IEC 20000 - An Introduction* provides thorough preparation for these exams.

For more information on Accredited Course Providers (ACPs), please check the websites of EXIN, ISEB and itSMF UK.

1.3.4   Most important terms and definitions
In its first section on the scope of the standard, ISO 20000-2 states:

> The variety of terms used for the same process, and between processes and functional groups (and job titles) can make the subject of Service Management confusing to the new manager. Failure to understand the terminology can be a barrier to establishing effective processes. Understanding the terminology is a tangible and significant benefit from ISO 20000. ISO 20000-2 recommends that service providers should adopt common terminology and a more consistent approach to Service Management. It gives a common basis for improvements in services. It also provides a framework for use by suppliers of Service Management tools.

ISO 20000-1 specifies the following terms and definitions:
* **Availability** - Ability of a component or service to perform its required function at a stated instant or over a stated period of time.
  NOTE: Availability is usually expressed as a ratio of the time that the service is actually available for use by the business to the agreed service hours.
* **Baseline** - Snapshot of the state of a service or individual configuration items at a point in time (see configuration item).
* **Change record** - Record containing details of which configuration items (see configuration item) are affected and how they are affected by an authorized change.
* **Configuration item (CI)** - Component of an infrastructure or an item which is, or will be, under the control of configuration management.
  NOTE: Configuration items may vary widely in complexity, size and type, ranging from an entire system including all hardware, software and documentation, to a single module or a minor hardware component.
* **Configuration management database (CMDB)** - Database containing all the relevant details of each configuration item and details of the important relationships between them.
* **Document** - Information and its supporting medium.

NOTE 1: In this standard, records (see record) are distinguished from documents by the fact that they function as evidence of activities, rather than evidence of intentions.

NOTE 2: Examples of documents include policy statements, plans, procedures, service level agreements and contracts.

- **Incident** - Any event which is not part of the standard operation of a service and which causes or may cause an interruption to, or a reduction in, the quality of that service.
- **Problem** - Unknown underlying cause of one or more incidents.
- **Record** - Document stating results achieved or providing evidence of activities performed.

  NOTE 1: In this standard, records are distinguished from documents by the fact that they function as evidence of activities, rather than evidence of intentions.

  NOTE 2: Examples of records include audit reports, requests for change, incident reports, individual training records and invoices sent to customers.[8]
- **Release** - Collection of new and/or changed configuration items which are tested and introduced into the live environment together.
- **Request for change** - Form or screen used to record details of a request for a change to any configuration item within a service or infrastructure.
- **Service desk** - Customer facing support group who do a high proportion of the total support work.
- **Service level agreement (SLA)** - Written agreement between a service provider and a customer that documents services and agreed service levels.
- **Service Management** - Management of services to meet the business requirements.
- **Service provider** - The organization aiming to achieve ISO 20000.

In this book, when using the term 'service provider', we automatically mean 'IT service provider', as ISO 20000 defines.

1.3.5 Scope

The service provider can demonstrate their ability to provide services that meet customer requirements by standardizing Service Management processes according to broadly accepted standards. The specification as applied in ISO 20000 represents an industry consensus on quality standards for IT Service Management processes. Part 1 of the standard defines what requirements a service provider shall meet in order to deliver managed services of an acceptable quality to customers.

Businesses may use it to:
- tender for services
- monitor if all service providers in a supply chain follow a consistent approach
- manage risk
- evaluate (the value of) services

Service providers can use it to:
- reduce the cost of their services
- monitor and improve their service quality
- benchmark their IT management Service Management activities

---

8 These records do not need to be paper records; they can be on digital media or other media as well.

- serve as the basis for an independent assessment
- demonstrate the ability to provide services that meet customer requirements
- improve service delivery through the effective application of processes to monitor and improve service quality

As ISO 20000 is process-based, it is not intended for product assessment. "However, organizations developing service management tools, products and systems may use both part 1 and 2 to help them develop tools, products and systems that support best practice service management", ISO 20000-1 states.

1.3.6   The quality management system process model

Subsection 1 of ISO 20000-1 contains a picture that shows "a number of closely related service management processes" (see Figure 1.1). These are the Service Management processes of ISO 20000, and constitute the product realization processes of the generic quality management systems standard ISO 9001:2000 (see Figure 1.3).

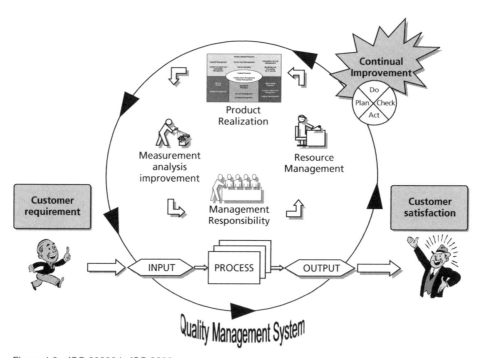

Figure 1.3   ISO 20000 in ISO 9000

Although ISO 20000-1 does address process interfaces, the standard does not specify relationships between the processes. One reason that the standard gives for this is that these relationships depend on the usage within an organization. The use of process modeling tools can aid the definition of process interfaces and the validation that the correct information is flowing through the process. Any framework may be used to integrate these processes; besides ITIL, which is the best known, proprietary models can also be used.

ISO 20000 describes three overarching management processes (see Figure 1.4):

- **management system:**
  - management responsibility (the standard's Section 3.1)
  - documentation requirements (the standard's Section 3.2)
  - competence, awareness and training (the standard's Section 3.3)
- **planning and implementing Service Management** (the standard's Section 4)
- **planning and implementing new or changed services** (the standard's Section 5)

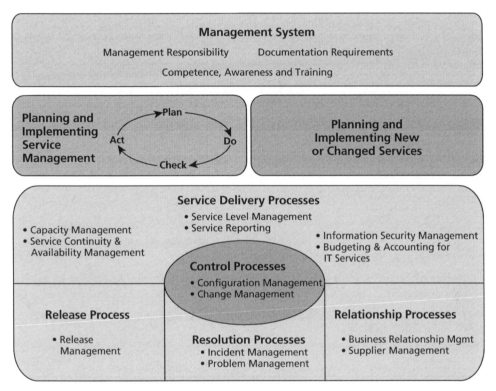

Figure 1.4   Overview ISO 20000 Service Management system

1.3.7   Requirements and objectives

This section summarizes the main objective, 'shalls' and 'shoulds' for each ISO 20000 process. The use of an imperative also indicates a 'shall'.

ISO 20000-1 requires a number of activities. It defines 170 'shalls', while ISO 9001 contains only 135 'shalls'. This publication concludes with a brief overview of the required documents and records.

Requirements for a management system

ISO 20000-1 requires "a management system, including policies and a framework to enable the effective management and implementation of all IT services". Management shall facilitate the framework needed to implement and maintain IT services. Their role and responsibilities shall be clear, and proper documentation shall be guaranteed. Furthermore, management shall:

- agree policies, goals and plans for IT management
- communicate the importance of the Service Management objectives
- ensure customer requirements are met
- appoint a member of management to be responsible for the co-ordination and management of all services (*senior responsible owner*);this role is responsible for ensuring that there is evidence of Service Management policies, plans and procedures
- provide resources to plan, implement, monitor, review and improve service delivery
- manage risks, and conduct Service Management reviews

For the *competence, awareness and training* part of the standard, staff shall be aware of their relevance within the wider business context, and how they contribute to the achievement of quality objectives. Determine the required competencies and responsibilities for each role and provide adequate training where required.

Planning and implementing Service Management

To develop a quality management system, an organization has to identify its purpose, define the policies and objectives, determine the processes and determine the sequence of these processes. This is called *Planning and implementing Service Management.*

To plan a process, an organization has to define the activities of the process according to the Plan-Do-Check-Act (PDCA) cycle (see Figure 1.5). The model assumes that to provide appropriate quality, the following steps must be undertaken repeatedly:

- **Plan** - Establish the objectives and processes necessary to deliver the results. This stage is completed with agreements that are measurable and realistic, and a plan of how they are to be achieved.
- **Do** - Implement the processes.
- **Check** - Monitor and measure processes and services against policies, objectives and requirements.
- **Act** - Identify actions to continually improve performance.

By iteratively progressing through this cycle, it can be assured that business and IT continue to align better (see Figure 1.6).

Documentation is important in successful application of the PDCA model. As the output of each activity is the input of the next activity in the model, a constant feedback is realized, and transparency in relationships between processes is created. 'Documentation' should not, however, be interpreted straight into more paperwork or be associated with more red tape. In essence, it is important that the information flow between the processes is defined, agreed upon, measurable and clear.

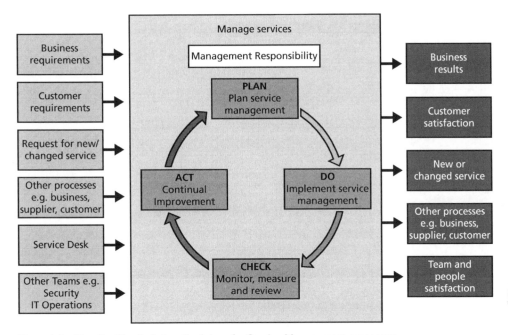

Figure 1.5   Plan-Do-Check-Act methodology for Service Management processes

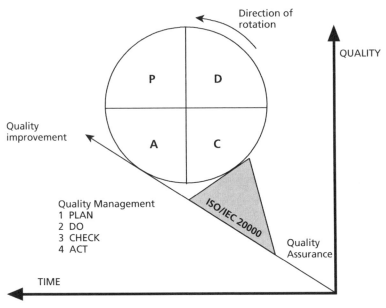

Figure 1.6   Deming's PDCA quality improvement cycle

Planning and implementing new or changed services

ISO 20000 has a separate process for *planning and implementing new or changed services*[9]. This is "to ensure that new services and changes to services will be deliverable and manageable at the agreed cost and service quality". Each new or changed service shall be introduced using the "planning and implementing service management" procedures. An impact analysis should provide insight into the cost, organizational, technical and commercial impact of any proposed new or changed service. This shall be carefully considered.

Service level management (SLM)

An organization's full range of services shall be agreed and documented in SLAs, as well as in supporting agreements, together with the corresponding targets. These agreements should be based on the customer's business needs, and shall be reviewed regularly and maintained under the control of the change management process.

The minimum content of an SLA should be (a reference to):
- description of service, service targets, communications and reporting
- authorization details
- validity period and/or SLA change control mechanism
- high level financial management details
- service provider liability and obligations such as security
- customer responsibilities such as security
- supporting and related services
- impact, urgency and priority guidelines
- service hours, date exceptions, critical business periods and out-of-hours cover
- workload limits (upper and lower), such as agreed number of users
- contact details of people authorized to act in case of emergencies
- actions to be taken in the event of a service interruption
- escalation and notification process
- scheduled and agreed interruptions
- complaints procedures
- housekeeping procedures (maintenance)
- exceptions to the terms given in the SLA
- glossary of terms

Service levels need to be monitored and reported against targets and trend reports, from a customer perspective. All non-conformances shall be reported and reviewed, in order to provide input to plans for improving the service.

Service reporting

Service reporting shall provide "agreed, reliable, timely and accurate reports" to provide an information platform for further action and future decisions. To this aim, each service report shall include:
- service identity
- service purpose

---

9 Implementing this process can minimize the gap between 'projects' and 'IT management'.

- service audience
- details of the data source
- details on performance against service level targets (also following major events)
- information on trends
- non compliance
- satisfaction analyses

Any good service report must also include the period or timeframe covered.

Service continuity and availability management

Agreed service continuity and availability commitments shall be met in all circumstances. Therefore, availability and service continuity requirements shall be identified on the basis of business plans, SLAs and risk assessments. These requirements shall include:
- access rights
- response times
- end-to-end availability of system components

To ensure these requirements can be met, an organization shall develop, test and maintain availability and service continuity plans.

Measure and record availability, investigate any unplanned non-availability and take appropriate actions. Where possible, predict potential issues and take preventive action.

Budgeting and accounting for IT services

ISO 20000-1 requires clear policies and processes for:
- budgeting and accounting for all service components
- apportioning indirect costs and allocating direct costs to services
- financial control and authorization

Financial control and decision-making shall be facilitated by budgeting costs in sufficient detail. The service provider shall:
- monitor and report costs against budget
- review the financial forecasts
- manage costs accordingly

The actual accounting practices in IT have to be aligned with the wider accountancy practices of the service provider. Charging is not covered by ISO 20000, as it is an optional activity.

Capacity management

The service provider shall have sufficient capacity to meet the current and future agreed demands of customer's business needs. To this aim, capacity management shall produce a capacity plan addressing the business needs. It should evaluate and adjust this plan at least annually, and whenever new services are included within the scope of the management system. It shall also identify and apply methods, procedures and techniques for monitoring, tuning and providing adequate service capacity. This includes being aware of new and changing technology. Finally, capacity management shall address changes in the required infrastructure, related to variations in business requirements, technology and the impact of external changes.

Information security management

An information security policy approved by management, with appropriate authority - and based on the overall business security policy - shall be communicated to all relevant parties. This is "to manage information security effectively within all service activities".

The requirements of the information security policy shall be implemented by security controls. These controls are also needed to manage risks associated with access to the service or systems. Document the controls and describe:
- risks to which the controls relate
- manner of operation and maintenance of the controls
- relation to implemented changes

Define procedures to ensure that:
- security incidents are reported and recorded in line with incident management procedures
- all security incidents are investigated and appropriate management actions are taken
- types, volumes and impacts of security incidents and malfunctions are monitored by adequate mechanisms
- actions for improvements identified during this process are recorded and provide input into a service improvement plan
- external access to systems and services is based on adequate formal agreements

Control and identify risks by creating an overview of all company assets. Also define who has access to them. Assign an owner to each asset. Risk assessments should be performed regularly, especially during changes.

Other ISO standards addressing security are ISO 27001 and ISO 27002 (called ISO 17799 prior to 2007). The first one specifies the requirements for a documented information security management system, whereas ISO 27002 provides guidance on information security management. Implementation of the requirements of ISO 20000-1 will not satisfy all the requirements that are necessary to obtain certification against ISO 27001. Organizations certified to ISO 27001 will more easily satisfy the security requirements within ISO 20000-1.

Business relationship management

A service provider shall identify and document the stakeholders and customers of its services, in order to establish and maintain a good relationship, based on understanding the business drivers. The service provider should plan and document interim meetings to discuss performance, achievements, issues and action plans. The organizations should follow up on agreed actions. The service provider should attend reviews at least annually, and before and after major changes, considering:
- changes in service scope
- SLAs and contracts
- current and projected business needs
- past performance

Define a formal complaints procedure with your customers, including:
* recording, investigating, and acting upon complaints
* reporting and formal closure of all complaints
* a procedure for escalation of outstanding complaints

Assign the responsibility for managing customer satisfaction and the business relationship process to one individual or individuals. Put a process in place for obtaining and acting upon feedback from regular customer satisfaction measurements. Variations in satisfaction levels should be investigated and understood. Use results of feedback and complaints analysis as input to the service improvement plan. Compliments should also be documented and reported to the service delivery team.

Supplier management
Third party suppliers shall be managed to ensure the provision of seamless, quality services. As a service provider, maintain for each service and supplier:
* a definition of services, scope, roles and responsibilities in SLAs or other similar documents
* alignment of supplier contracts with the SLAs of the service provider's business
* clearly documented roles and relationships between lead and subcontracted suppliers
* review of contracts and changes to the contract and SLAs
* a formal process to deal with contractual disputes and (un)expected end of the service; disputes should be recorded, investigated, acted upon and formally closed

A service provider shall also ensure that all contract (SLA) changes are in line with the change management process, and monitor and review performance against service level targets. Furthermore, the service provider shall identify and record actions for improvement and pass them on to its service improvement plan.

It shall be clear whether the service provider is dealing with all suppliers directly, or if a lead supplier is taking responsibility for subcontract suppliers. The service provider shall obtain evidence that lead suppliers are formally managing subcontracted suppliers, guided by the requirements of ISO 20000-1. This means that lead suppliers shall be able to demonstrate processes to ensure that subcontracted suppliers meet contractual requirements.

In most cases there will be several suppliers, sometimes divided into lead and subcontracted suppliers (see Figure 1.7). In order to tune suppliers and internal services, the service provider is charged with managing the relationships, (underpinning) contracts and deliverable services. The service provider shall have documented supplier management processes, and shall appoint a contract manager responsible for the relationship with each supplier.

Incident management
The goal of this process is to restore agreed service to the business as soon as possible, or to respond to service requests. To this aim, adopt procedures defining:
* business impact
* recording and prioritization (based on impact and urgency)
* classification, updating, escalation

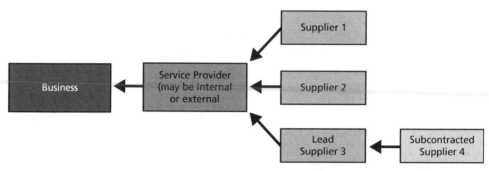

Figure 1.7   Example of relationship between service providers and suppliers

- communication to users about status of incidents
- resolution and formal closure

There should be a clear definition of a major incident and who is empowered to invoke changes to the normal operation of the incident and problem management process. A major incident should have a clearly defined responsible manager co-ordinating and controlling all aspects for the resolution. Classify and manage major incidents according to a defined process, taking into account:
- priority based on impact and urgency
- skills available
- resolution (providing service continuity)
- escalation if necessary
- updating and formal closure of incident record

Also keep the customers informed of the progress of their reported incidents or service requests. Alert them in advance if agreed service levels cannot be met. Make sure all staff involved in incident management have access to relevant information, such as known errors, problem resolutions and the configuration management database (CMDB).

Problem management
Problem management aims to minimize disruption to the business, by proactive identification and analysis of the cause of incidents, and by managing problems to closure. To this aim, adopt procedures to identify, minimize or avoid the impact of incidents and problems. Define:
- recording and classification of all problems
- updating of all problems
- escalation, resolution and closure of all problems

Furthermore managing problems shall include:
- reviewing to reduce problems by prevention; for example, by following trend analysis of incident volumes and types
- passing required changes to change management
- monitoring, reviewing and reporting of problem resolutions
- providing up-to-date information on known errors and corrected problems to incident management
- providing input to the service improvement plan

Unsolved or unusual problems with a high impact should be reviewed, to analyze trends and to provide input to other processes, such as customer or service desk education requirements. Education should also be part of problem prevention.

Configuration management

Components of the service and infrastructure need to be defined and controlled. This is the purpose of configuration management. It shall also maintain accurate configuration information and constitute an integrated approach to change and configuration management planning. Information on the impact of a requested change for the service and infrastructure shall be provided to the change management process.

Configuration audit and control procedures are to ensure and maintain the integrity and relevance of systems, services and service components. They shall include:
• recording deficiencies
• methods on improvement actions
• reporting on the outcome

A configuration plan should include:
• scope, objectives, policy, roles and responsibilities
• definition, recording and reporting of configuration items
• requirements for accountability, traceability and auditability
• configuration control information, such as the owner of the configuration item, and version and release control

The following items should be registered in the configuration management database (CMDB):
• issues and releases of systems and software and related documentation, such as requirements specifications and test reports
• configuration baselines or build statements for applicable environment, standard hardware builds and releases
• master hardcopy and electronic libraries
• licenses and security components, such as firewalls
• service related documentation such as SLAs
• service supporting facilities such as power to the computer room
• relationships and dependencies between configuration items and the supported services

Change management

Change management assesses, approves, reviews and co-ordinates the implementation of all changes in a controlled manner. To this end, all changes shall be recorded and classified (eg urgent, major, minor, etc.). The process shall also provide procedures, which include:
• a defined and documented scope for all service and infrastructural changes
• assessment of changes for risks, impact and business benefits
• the manner in which unsuccessful changes shall be reversed or remedied
• policies and procedures for emergency changes
• change scheduling, monitoring and reporting
• approval, checking, scheduling and controlling of the implementation of changes
• a post implementation review, which should check whether:

- the change met its objectives
- the customers are satisfied with the results
- there have been any unexpected side effects

Feed the results of the post implementation review into the service improvement plans.

In order to detect increasing levels of change, analyze change records regularly for frequently recurring change categories, emerging trends and other relevant information.

Maintain and communicate a schedule containing details of all the changes approved for implementation and their proposed implementation dates. The people affected by the change should receive accurate scheduling information.

Release management

The objective of release management is to deliver, distribute and track one or more changes in a release into the live environment. To facilitate this, document and agree upon the release policy. This shall state the frequency and type of releases, in order to deliver, distribute and track one or more changes in a release into the live environment. The release policy should define:
- the roles and responsibilities
- the authority for releasing versions into acceptance, test and production environments
- the unique identification, description, verification and acceptance of all releases
- the approach to grouping changes into a release
- the approach to automating the build, installation and release distribution processes to aid repeatability and efficiency

As a service provider, plan the release of services, systems, software and hardware. Consult all relevant parties for the roll-out plan. These include customers, users, and operations and support staff. The roll-out plan shall include:
- records of release date and deliverables
- references to related change requests, known errors and problems
- method for remedying the release if unsuccessful
- communication to incident management

ISO 20000-1 states the release management process should be integrated with the configuration and change management processes. Make sure all documentation on new releases meets the CMDB requirements. Update the asset and configuration management records after successful installation. The release management process should allow change management to execute a post-implementation review and feed recommendations into the service improvement plan.

Measures to be monitored for this process include:
- successful releases
- failed releases
- incidents related to releases

Design and implement release and distribution in such a manner that the integrity of hardware and software is maintained. Establish a controlled acceptance test environment to build and test all releases prior to distribution. Verification and acceptance processes should verify and ensure that:

- the controlled acceptance test environment matches the requirements of target production environments
- the release is created from versions under configuration management control
- the testing has been completed to the satisfaction of customers and service provider staff
- the release authority signs off each stage of acceptance testing
- the target platform satisfies the hardware and software prerequisites

1.3.8 Documentation, processes, procedures and records required

With regard to documentation, processes, procedures and records, Section 3.2 of ISO 20000-1 states:

> Service providers shall provide documents and records to ensure effective planning, operation and control of Service Management. This shall include:
> a) documented Service Management policies and plans
> b) documented service level agreements
> c) documented processes and procedures required by this standard
> d) records required by this standard
>
> Procedures and responsibilities shall be established for the creation, review, approval, maintenance, disposal and control of the various types of documents and records.
>
> NOTE: The documentation can be in any form or type of medium.[10]

As in any ISO/IEC standard, all processes described in Part 1 are mandatory for the subject of an audit. They all have to have documents and records, including a process description. Without having the supporting documents and records it is impossible to check all mandatory processes for compliance to their description, and for the effectiveness and efficiency. An organization is free to design additional processes and procedures to meet requirements of ISO 20000-1.

ISO does not define the term 'procedure', but does require "documented and maintained procedures for each process or set of processes" (Section 4.2, implement Service Management and provide the services). The ITIL version 3 glossary definition of a procedure is:

> A **procedure** is a document containing steps that specify how to achieve an activity. Procedures are defined as part of processes.

So, when describing the processes, the procedures should also be described. In addition, there are some additional procedures related to the scope of this standard, but outside the processes mentioned, such as, an audit process or procedure. Table 1.2 provides some explicitly stated processes and procedures, but this should be read with the above in mind, as it can never be exhaustive.

---

10 For example, electronic or optical discs, photos, a master copy of software or an intranet website.

(sub)section part 1	process or procedure required
3.2 Documentation requirements	documentation procedures
4.2 Implement service management and provide the services (Do)	documented and maintained procedures for each process or set of processes
4.3 Monitoring, measuring and reviewing (Check)	conduct audits
4.4 Continual improvement (Act)	improve service management
6.1 Service level management	supporting SLA procedures
6.4 Budgeting and accounting for IT services	budget and account for all components apportion indirect costs and allocate direct costs to services control finances and authorize effectively
6.5 Capacity management	monitor service capacity tune service performance provide adequate capacity
6.6 Information security management	investigate all security incidents take management action
7.2 Business relationship management	complaints process customer satisfaction process
7.3 Supplier management	manage supplier - conduct a major contract review - deal with contractual disputes - deal with end of service subcontractor lead supplier processes
8.2 Incident management	manage impact of incidents define the recording, prioritization, business impact, classification, updating, escalation, resolution and formal closure of all incidents
8.3 Problem management	identify, minimize or avoid the impact of incidents and problems
9.1 Configuration management	ensure that the integrity of systems, services and service components are maintained recording deficiencies, initiating corrective actions and reporting
9.2 Change management	control the authorization and implementation of emergency changes
10.1 Release management	updating and changing of configuration information and change records

Table 1.2   Processes or procedures required by ISO 20000-1

Service providers shall provide **documentation and records** to support the management processes, such as:
- policies and plans
- service level agreements (SLAs)
- procedures and processes
- records required by ISO 20000

Establish **procedures and responsibilities** for the creation, review, approval, maintenance, disposal and control of documents and records. The senior responsible owner should ensure that evidence is available for an audit of Service Management policies, plans and procedures. A process for creating and managing documents should be operational. Documentation should also be protected from damage.

As with processes or procedures, not many required documents are specified in ISO 20000. Again, however, this does not mean that an organization, having established only the explicitly required documents, will automatically be certified against the standard. As Section 4.2 of the standard states, they shall be able to prove they have firmly established all processes required by the standard, being also able to show the documentation necessary for this (once again, not necessarily on paper).

Special kinds of documents in ISO standards are **records**. Records are documents stating results achieved or providing evidence of activities performed (please refer to Section 1.3.4, terminology, for more information).

Gaining certification to ISO 20000 should really be the side effect of an organization wide Service Management improvement culture that continually strives to improve on the existing capability and adheres to best practice at all times within the confines of the requirements of the standard.

1.4   Benefits and costs

1.4.1   Operational benefits
As a side effect of ISO 20000 certification, service operation will normally become more efficient and effective, as a result of the focus on continual service improvement and the adoption of consistent repeatable processes, roles and responsibilities.

1.4.2   Management benefits
Improved quality of management information, improved financial and operational planning and clear responsibilities are all benefits that the Service Provider's management team will enjoy as a result of implementing ISO 20000.

The business management team will also realize benefits through enhanced business products and services that rely on IT service provision and delivery. These may be enhanced in many ways, including reliability, functionality and performance.

As can be seen in the NCS' case study later in this book, they have achieved real efficiency gains through reducing the amount of re-work and have also been able to re-deploy their staff, making best use of their skills and experience.

1.4.3   Business benefits
Certification to the standard will also lead to benefits for the business; this is a prime focus for ISO 20000. There are many indirect benefits, some of which are highlighted here:
• By having an IT service provider to predictably manage the introduction of new services, businesses can plan ahead with confidence for new product launches that require IT support.

- Business priorities and policies will be a prime consideration for the IT service provider; this will contribute to maintaining and improving customer satisfaction.
- The IT service provider will work closely with the business to understand their plans, in order to be more responsive to their needs.
- By having an enhanced relationship with the business, the IT service provider will be in a good position to help to contribute to business decisions, by providing valuable information on how IT Service Management can support them. Conversely, they will help to influence business requirements that may otherwise lead to time consuming and costly work, which may have a small disproportionate benefit, hence leading to cost reductions for the business.

Customers will find that, by following ISO 20000, their service providers are more aligned to meeting the needs of the business, and more able to meet their service requirements. The standard impacts on the whole of the service providers organization, through which best practice will permeate, thereby improving service delivery.

> Nippon's IT Service Management department found that their customers felt that they were working closer with them and able to provide information to enable informed decision-making regarding service provision.

1.4.4 Costs
The costs of attaining and retaining certification will vary from service provider to service provider. Many influencing factors are involved, including:
- **Scope of the certification** - If the scope of certification is wide, then the time to assess and audit the capability will increase. Additionally, there may need to be more investment made to ensure that the management system remains robust across the full scope. Please refer to Section 1.3.5 for further information on defining the scope.
- **Size of the service provider** - For a larger service provider the cost is likely to be higher given the sheer scale of operation. However, they may realize economies of scale given the number of employees used when compared to a smaller organization.
- **Complexity and criticality of the service provider's services and the business being supported** - A more complex and critical environment will demand increased management focus and governance, to ensure that the services remain operable to the needs of the business.
- **Skills and experience available** - A commonly overlooked aspect, many skills are required during and after the certification process. There are obviously operational and management roles following certification, but the costs can also multiply exponentially leading up to certification, if a service provider is advised in a poor or inefficient way, either by its internal staff or by external consultants.
- **Current level of capability** - One service provider may be more capable than another; thus they could be nearer, or have even surpassed the requirements of ISO 20000, and may have less to do to achieve certification, hence costs would be reduced.
- **Certified to ISO 9000 already** - A service provider that has already achieved certification to ISO 9000, covering at least the scope of the ITSM function, will find it easier to demonstrate alignment to the Requirements for a Management System (Section 3 of the standard) and Planning and Implementing Service Management (Section 4 of the standard) in particular.

Costs in this area will therefore be reduced significantly, although the context of applying these aspects within the IT Service Management arena needs to be shown.
- **Certified to ISO 27001 already** - The same applies to a service provider who already has ISO 27001 certification. They will find it easier to demonstrate alignment to the Information Security Management requirements (Section 6.6 of the standard) in particular.

Considering these and other factors, the primary costs will include the following:
- **consultancy costs** - to provide expert experienced help, if necessary
- **training costs** - to enable staff to understand what is required of them and how they can contribute to certification and retention
- **process improvement costs** - where gaps or issues have been identified that should have been bridged already by the service provider, irrespective of whether or not they were looking to achieve certification to ISO 20000
- **tool costs** - where the current tools are hindering certification
- **project costs** - where a project manager is used (this is highly recommended), there will be resource costs and perhaps project management tool costs, which will need to be accounted for; there may also be additional costs associated with establishing a project team to perform, for example, technical authorship of documents to support certification
- **registered certification body audit costs** - in order for a recognized certificate to be awarded based upon industry standards

These are explored in more detail in Chapter 2, but as can be seen, there is no simple answer to the question 'how much is ISO 20000 certification going to cost?'

Keep in mind, though, that the costs need to be considered in the context of the benefits. Poor service costs money, and there will inevitably be cost savings if certification to the standard is achieved.

In addition to the one-off costs described here, on-going costs should be accounted for in order to maintain the certification. These should be limited to the costs surrounding the surveillance and re-certification audits performed by the Registered Certification Body, as all other activities should be part of normal IT Service Management practices. However, in practice, there could be on-going costs associated with initially bridging the gaps that the service provider will need to address within its operational expenditure budgets.

> EDS' quality managers estimated it wouldn't cost large amounts of extra time or money on top of the costs for the ISO 9001 implementation.

1.5   Perspectives on ISO 20000 Implementation

1.5.1   Customer's perspective

A fundamental principle of the standard is that the service provider needs to be aligned to the needs of the customer where an agreement has been reached between the two parties. There are references throughout the standard to this alignment which will ultimately bring significant benefit to the customer; these are summarized below:

- **Requirements for a Management System (Section 3):**
  - Senior business and service provider representatives meet to discuss plans and strategies.
  - Service providers contribute to the overall business case.
- **Planning and Implementing Service Management (Section 4):**
  - There is business representation, considering the impact of continual improvement.
  - Service improvement plans are aligned to business needs.
- **Planning and Implementing New or Changed Services (Section 5):**
  - Possible and probable business needs are identified alongside definite needs.
  - Service acceptance criteria are defined to include business requirements.
- **Service Level Management and Service Reporting (Section 6.1 and 6.2):**
  - Realistic service level agreement targets are aligned with service provider capability.
  - SLA and service reporting are defined in a way that is relevant to the customer.
- **Service Continuity and Availability Management (Section 6.3):**
  - Initiatives are prioritized by business 'value add'.
  - Cost of unavailability in business terms are known for each service.
- **Budgeting and Accounting for IT Services (Section 6.4):**
  - There is demonstrable business involvement in service provider financial decisions.
  - The service provider budgeting is integrated with business budgeting.
- **Capacity Management (Section 6.5):**
  - The capacity plan has been aligned to business predictions.
  - There is a regular feed of business data into capacity management.
- **Information Security Management (Section 6.6):**
  - Service provider security controls are aligned with business security policies.
  - The service provider understands the value of business information.
- **Business Relationship Management (Section 7.2):**
  - There are regular meetings, soliciting future planning information.
  - There is communication, to the appropriate areas within the service provider's business, of information gathered from the business.
- **Supplier Management (Section 7.3):**
  - Education, awareness and alignment are focused on end-customer's needs.
  - Review of performance is based upon business-focused objectives.
- **Incident and Problem Management (Section 8.2 and 8.3):**
  - Definition of categories and priorities are steered by the business.
  - Staff understand the business context of each service.
- **Configuration Management (Section 9.1):**
  - Business data owners are involved in design.
  - Status accounting reports regarding business configuration items are aligned to requirements.
  - Verification and audit are co-ordinated with the business.
  - Close alignment with business continuity/asset management is ensured.
- **Change Management (Section 9.2):**
  - Active business involvement in the Change Advisory Board is ensured.
  - Clear communication of the Forward Schedule of Change to the business takes place.
- **Release Management (Section 10.1):**
  - Shared prioritization of release content takes place.

The *end user* will benefit in similar ways to the customer; they will generally perceive an improved service that is more responsive to their needs.

1.5.2 Supplier's perspective

Although suppliers to the service provider are not involved in the certification audit process itself, their behavior and processes will contribute to the ease of the certification process for the service provider in this area, by ensuring an end-to-end integrated focus on Service Management.

Suppliers will be more accurately managed, given the requirement for a supplier management process. This will help them to understand their role within the service provider's supply chain, and to optimize their behavior. This will also be of benefit to them. Suppliers will also see other benefits:

- They will be more actively involved in contributing to the definition of the process touchpoints between themselves and the service provider.
- They will work more closely with the service provider on continual service improvement initiatives.
- They will have access to future planning information, where available, to help them to manage the scope of their services.
- They will benefit from service providers adopting robust processes.

In conclusion, the supplier will experience a tighter integration with the service provider.

1.5.3 Service Provider's perspective

One of the common misconceptions about ISO 20000 implementation is that any gaps identified during an assessment are only being bridged because the standard says they shall be bridged. The standard only documents the minimum that is required in order for service providers to operate in a way that works for itself, its suppliers and, most importantly, its customers. Any gaps that need to be bridged are shortfalls in what is expected for normal quality service provision from the service provider. The main benefit and impact for the service provider's employees is that it allows them to work in a successful, achieving team, and to feel a sense of achievement themselves.

The standard also benefits employees by requiring competency, awareness and training. A service provider may have the best processes and tools, but if they do not have the right people to define, operate and maintain them, then they will not achieve the agreed needs of their customers and end users.

Employees may well see their role profiles change as part of the overall continual service improvement program. This may include links to competencies that are required to fulfill the roles.

Due to a better alignment of business and IT, the service provider's employees may experience an improvement in how they are perceived by the business staff, resulting in a better working relationship.

All in all, the employee should see a positive effect on their work environment.

To ensure that these actions take place, it is necessary to have a strong organizational change management team in place, right from the beginning of the process.

Further benefits for the Service Provider as a whole can be seen in Section 2.6 'Set Up Business Case'.

1.5.4   Differences between organizations

Depending upon the type of service provider, ISO 20000 certification can lead in addressing different challenges and realizing different benefits. Table 1.3 provides some examples of the different, though similar in nature, considerations that service providers may have, based upon common topics.

Finally, the size of the organization will also play a part in the ISO 20000 certification process, particularly in the design phase. For a smaller service provider, they will be able to consolidate processes under a small number of managers, whilst larger service providers will have to have at least one manager per process or sometimes, for geographically distributed service provider structures, even a number of process managers, working with the governance of a process owner.

> The **key message** when considering ISO 20000 certification is: "Understand why you are looking at ISO 20000 certification and what internal and external influences you have before going too far down the certification route, as this approach will help to steer your certification and retention strategy."

Topic	Internal service provider (ISP)	External service provider (ESP)
Certification vs compliance	Are more likely to comply to the standard than ultimately gain certification, although they will soon realize that certification will help with on-going conformance to the standard.	Are more likely to certify as they will want to demonstrate their achievement through an independent audit allowing them to capitalize on the marketing potential.
Legal and regulatory	For public sector, government based ISPs in particular, they will be subject to many legal and regulatory requirements in terms of how they conduct their business.

For private sector based ISPs they will be closer, for example, to regulatory requirements being placed on their internal customers, and will need to work ever more closely to support on-going compliance. | External service providers are generally more liable to legal and regulatory requirements; for example, they could be listed on the US NASDAQ stock exchange and therefore be subject to the Sarbanes-Oxley Act, which, while it could also apply to ISPs, will permeate through an ESP's business more thoroughly. In Europe, the EU 8th Directive also provides similar IT requirements to that of Sarbanes-Oxley. |
| **Management system** | Will typically have one management system for providing services to its internal customers. The certification scope will therefore be easier to define for the ISP. | Will have multiple external customers who demand specific ways of providing their services, which quite often leads to multiple management systems. The ESP will therefore need to consider how it consolidates these or how it specifies its scope of certification more closely. |
| **Marketing** | Certification could be used to promote the capability of the ISP with its internal customers and help to delay or stop potential outsourcing. Also helps to promote the use of best practices within ISPs. | Will be high up on the agenda, helping to differentiate it from its commercial competitors. |
| **Other existing certifications** | If they have any existing certification it is likely to be against ISO 9001, but generally the standards playing field will be less populated and therefore less complex for an ISP. | Are more likely to have multiple certification to standards for differing scopes. This can confuse the matter when trying to achieve ISO 20000 certification as it could be assumed that achievement of one certification (such as ISO 27001) will provide immunity to be re-audited for common elements in ISO 20000. The fact of the matter is that ISO 20000 stands alone, but the ESP could benefit from other certifications as it may be nearer to conformance to ISO 20000.

Management systems for quality, information security and IT Service Management can and should be integrated into one single system. Certification Bodies in general can combine (certification) audits, reducing the impact that an audit may have on an organization. **PAS 99:2006** 'Specification of Common Management System Requirements as a Framework for Integration' provides further detail on this approach. |

Table 1.3   Considerations for different types of service providers

Topic	Internal service provider (ISP)	External service provider (ESP)
Strategy	Are going to be more likely to have an elective strategy towards certification, where the scope of certification is going to be more all encompassing than their ESP counterparts.	Are more likely to have their certification scope dictated to them by their external customers who are requiring the ESP to become certified for the management system supporting the services being provided to the customer. This is normally accompanied with a timescale. ESPs are therefore more likely to have multiple ISO 20000 certifications for different customers if the management system is different per customer.

Table 1.3   Considerations for different types of service providers

Chapter 2
The road to certification: planning and preparation

2.1 Commitment of the service provider

2.1.1 Management commitment

One of the most refreshing aspects of the standard can be found within the 'Requirements for a management system' and 'Planning and implementing service management' sections.

Some requirements state that the senior management team need to take action themselves, rather than simply asking their staff to do the work.

In reality, this can be one of the major selling points for the day-to-day operational staff, who welcome the closer alignment of what they do within the overall context of the IT Service Management organization.

As with most initiatives, management commitment is one of the most important aspects that must be addressed at the start of the ISO 20000 strategy, during the preparation for the certification process and beyond the certification award. In addition to the management team supporting the certification process by doing what the standard requires of them, they need to provide the following support and commitment:
- **During the certification process:**
  - *Drivers* - It is important for the IT Service Management team to articulate and understand the reasons why they are considering certification to the standard. This can help to set a focus for the program, and influence the methods and techniques used to address any capability gaps against the requirements of the standard.
  - *Costs* - A frequently asked question is 'how much will ISO 20000 certification cost our organization?' Perhaps the more appropriate question should be 'how much could ISO 20000 save our organization?' The answer to both of these questions can only be determined once a capability assessment has been made of the current situation. This will provide a baseline that can be compared against the target minimum position, as defined by the standard. Any data can be used to identify both the direct benefits from certification

and the costs of certification to address the shortfall. Indirect benefits such as enhanced marketing capability can also be derived; these will be discussed in Section 2.4.2.

– *Time and resources* - Although the requirements of ISO 20000 are common sense and should be performed as part of the ITSM professional's regular duties, quite often there are areas that are missing or need refinement. These changes require time to improve, and could result in a significant step change, as opposed to refinement. It may not be possible for a single individual to execute a significant step change; instead it may require a (small) dedicated team. Another approach is to allow the individuals concerned to have the dedicated time to contribute to the changes needed, prior to embedding the changes within the organization.

• **Beyond certification award:**

– *Continual alignment* - All too often service providers focus on achieving certification rather than on retaining certification. The latter requires an emphasis on embedding within the organization the changes that lead to and enable the certification process. These changes must be maintained, and continual alignment to the standard and the Service Management plan demonstrated.

– *Supporting Staff* - Service Management without people is like a body without a heart. The people must be supported to enable them to do their job. Occasionally, there is a mismatch between the expectations of the management team and their staff, regarding what the staff believe they are being asked to do. This expectation should be clearly documented and support mechanisms put in place, such as a Continual Professional Development (CPD) Program and Mentoring Scheme.

> With regard to time and resources, EDS took the approach that all of their employees should see quality as a regular part of their job, so no extra hours or budget were assigned.

2.1.2 Awareness

'Awareness', or having knowledge of, is one term but 'understanding' and 'applying' help to complete the picture for an individual. Simply being aware of what is required of ones self is not enough to contribute to the certification process. However, if information is not clearly articulated, then the foundations for certification may be jeopardized. To be aware of, to understand and to apply the knowledge, are all critical elements. For example, the ability to be a good 'thought leader' or 'strategist' needs to be complemented with the ability to 'execute the plan'.

The information and the level of detail that needs to be communicated will depend upon the audience. For example, the needs of the network engineer will differ from those of a service manager. This should be considered when defining the communication plan. Figure 2.1 provides an indication of the information that should be considered for communication during and beyond certification.

2.1.3 Project organization

A service provider needs a structured way of achieving ISO 20000 certification and ultimately retaining it. Care should be taken that the message is not 'this is an ISO 20000 project', but rather 'this is a continual service improvement project' as that should be the focus; certification will follow as a secondary effect.

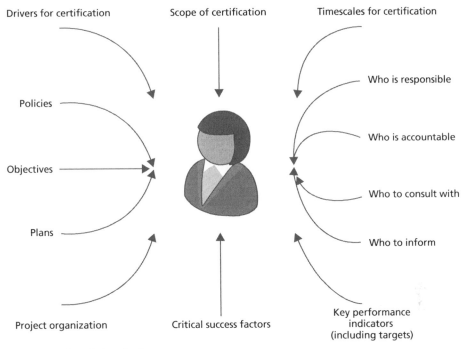

Drivers for certification

Scope of certification

Timescales for certification

Policies

Objectives

Plans

Project organization

Critical success factors

Who is responsible

Who is accountable

Who to consult with

Who to inform

Key performance indicators (including targets)

Figure 2.1   Knowledge sharing

Projects allow a more predictable result to be achieved in a more efficient and effective way.

The project organization itself needs to be structured representing key roles. Each service provider will, in practice, have its own project management methodology, perhaps based on PRINCE2™ or PMBoK®. Figure 2.2 provides a typical project organization structure.

The **project board** establishes the parameters within which the team will operate, including project tolerances. They also provide guidance and direction to the project, including the definition of the scope of certification. It is suggested that Business Representatives are included, to ensure that the focus on delivering and operating a service within the business context is not lost. They can also provide valuable insight and clarification into the strategic direction of the business.

The **project manager** is responsible for preparing plans, allocating work to assigned staff, and also monitors and controls progress. Depending upon the size of the project and organization, they may be supported by an administrative function, to assist with maintenance of plans and production of project related documents.

It is critical that there is a focus on the complete integrated picture for IT Service Management; therefore a **design authority** role is essential to ensure that the service design is customer-focused, integrated, takes account of supplier relationships and embraces a continual improvement philosophy.

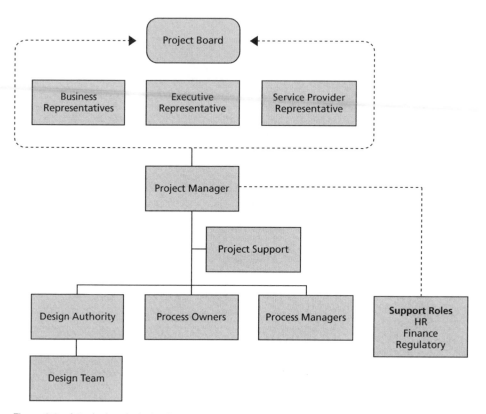

Figure 2.2   A typical project structure

The design authority may be supported by a **design team** who can perform the technical authorship of documents as required. Quite often this team will be dedicated to the activities. The benefits of this approach include:
- consistency of documentation
- higher probability of taking an integrated approach across functions
- conflicting operational priorities will be sidelined, helping to expedite any significant step change improvements

Process owners are required to co-ordinate the various functions and work activities at all levels of a process. This person will have the authority to make changes to the process as required, and manages the entire process cycle to ensure performance effectiveness. They may not manage the day-to-day activities. These are undertaken by the **process manager** (who could also be the line manager of the staff, and would also need to be involved) who will ensure conformance to the defined process.

The key differences between the two roles are as follows:
- The '**process owner**':
  - defines the scope and purpose of the process
  - determines required level of performance
  - sets improvement objectives and agrees priorities

– ensures that performance is monitored and reviewed
– allocates any resources required
– communicates goals and objectives
– ensures the process is defined and mapped
- The '**process manager**':
    – works with the 'process owner' to agree measures and targets
    – manages day-to-day operation of the process
    – highlights and implements continual service improvement opportunities

Finally, various **support roles** will play a part in the certification process. For example, ensuring compliance to corporate finance policies will assist ISO 20000 certification, as the standard recommends that the service provider should be aligned to wider accountancy practices.

Remember that the roles below the project board in Figure 2.2 may be combined if the service provider and project are small enough to deem this acceptable.

> Nippon established a well structured project organization with members selected from each of their divisions to support implementing ISO/IEC 20000 for the service range.

2.2   Commitment from other parties

2.2.1   Suppliers
ISO 20000 does not require suppliers to become certified to the standard in order to enable a service provider to become certified (see Figure 2.3).

The focus of the standard is on ensuring that the service provider, whether they are an internal service provider (ISP) or an external service provider (ESP), is managing the whole IT service provision on behalf of the End User Organization (EUO). The standard does not prevent delegation of activities to suppliers; however, it does expect that the service provider retains management control of all processes within the scope of ISO 20000 Part 1. There are six tests that contribute to this:
1. Is the service provider controlling and owning the process definition?
2. Does the service provider have the authority to require process compliance?
3. Can the service provider provide evidence of the execution of the process?
4. Does the service provider have control and ownership of the definition of services?
5. Is the service provider controlling and owning the Service Management plan?
6. Is the service provider controlling and owning improvements to the service?

The standard requires that the service provider has a Supplier Management process in place. The scope of this process should at least cover those suppliers that directly contribute to the service lifecycle.

The requirements that specifically reference the lead supplier can be addressed by the service provider, by including references within the contract(s) between the two organizations; for example, these clauses could state that:

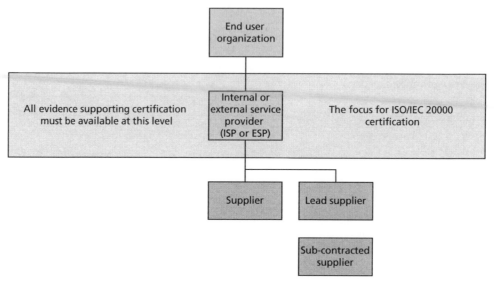

Figure 2.3   ISO 20000 Certification Focus

- The lead supplier must ensure that they clearly define and retain management control of the relationships between themselves and their sub-contracted suppliers.
- The lead supplier must be able to show that their sub-contracted suppliers are performing against their contractual commitments.
- Upon request, information relating to the lifecycle of these requirements must be made available to the service provider.

In summary, the lead supplier is expected to support the service in line with the commitments that they have made to the service provider; these commitments should be aligned to the needs of the EUO by the service provider. This alignment of commitment is often referred to as 'backing off' or 'flowing down' contractual requirements.

2.2.2   External regulations

It should be emphasized that compliance or certification with the standard does not in itself confer immunity from legal obligations. There are no clauses that require the service provider to align to particular legislation; however, they are expected to consider legislative changes, for example, in the capacity management process. However, a company complying to ISO 20000 is likely to be able to comply to many kinds of regulations, given the fact that the company is in control of its processes.

2.3   Determine goals

The standard can be used in many ways, including:
- as a baseline to comply with, without external ratification
- as a baseline to certify to under a recognized certification scheme
- as a reference for organizations initiating tenders

Compliance versus certification is a common conundrum. Why go to the expense of certification when self-audited compliance will do? Unfortunately, in today's business climate, telling someone that you are providing an integrated customer-focused experience is not as acceptable as an independent authoritative body doing the same. This independent body can identify issues that a service provider finds difficult to see, as they may be too close to the issue. Indeed, the benefit of certification goes much further than that; it tells others that the service provider is confident in their service provision being consistent and repeatable. It also provides an added incentive for process compliance, 'if we don't comply with the process, then we will lose certification' and all of the benefits that have been gained. All too often service providers establish a CobiT® or ITIL® process improvement program, to initially gain benefit, but then lose momentum because the changes are not embedded and part of the daily work ethic.

The challenge for certification is that the itSMF UK certification scheme is predicated on the service provider providing evidence that all of the requirements have been achieved and will continue to be achieved. This can be quite a significant task and it may take service providers many months to be ready for initial certification.

2.4   Determine scope

2.4.1   Organization, locations, services
The area which enjoys the most potential for initial debate when involved in an ISO 20000 program is that of scope. In this context, scope refers to the part, or whole, of IT Service Management that can be delimited by a number of factors:
- their customers
- their services
- their geography
- their organizational units

The example shown in Figure 2.4 highlights that it is the management system itself (of a fictional company 'FEDD Grand Prix'), that is the focus of certification as applied to the scope of:
- *their customers* - internal
- *their services* - IT infrastructure
- *their geography* - EMEA region
- *their organizational units* - ITSM team A

An appropriate scoping statement that ties all of this together would be:

> "The IT Service Management system that supports the provision of IT infrastructure services to internal customers within the technical and organizational boundaries of FEDD Grand Prix's ITSM Team A within the EMEA region. This is in accordance with FEDD Grand Prix's service catalogue and includes all IT Service Management processes and the management control of those interfaces that support them."

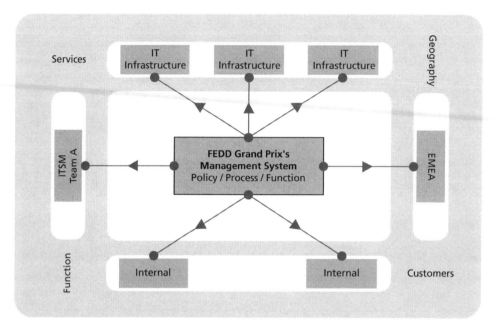

Figure 2.4   ITSM management system as applied to a scope

This scoping statement implies that there will be areas that will not be reviewed while auditing the management system; for example, services which are deemed non-IT infrastructure will not be included in the audit of the management system.

An example from the **Fujitsu FIP case study** can be found in Figure 2.5. Fujitsu's approach was to achieve certification for its Outsourcing Services Group's management system. This was partly driven by the desire to achieve independent recognition of its capabilities and also to provide a differentiator to commercial competitors.

Fujitsu FIP's scoping statement is:
The Service Management system supporting the **outsourced services** managed from the **Kanagawa office** (including Hosting and Housing Services, Network Services, Business Process Operation Services, Operation Management Services, Electronic Commerce Service and Application Services Provision Services).

It is very important to ensure that scoping statements are clearly expressed and are unambiguous. Any person who is viewing scoping statements with a view to working with an ISO 20000 certified service provider, should follow this up by requesting further detail regarding the statement, as it cannot possibly provide the entire picture in a single paragraph.

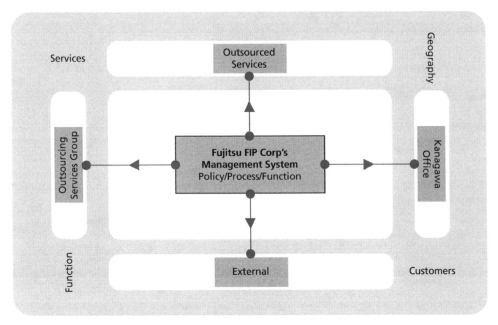

Figure 2.5   Fujitsu FIP Corporation's ISO 20000 Scope

Consideration should be made of future activities when setting the scoping statement. For example, if additional services are likely to be added to the service catalogue or indeed removed, then service providers should consider simply referring to the service catalogue in the scoping statement as opposed to listing specific services. This is predicated on the assumption that all of the services listed in the service catalogue are being managed through the one management system that has been identified.

For further explanation of scope and eligibility, see the websites of the National Accreditation Bodies or the itSMF UK guidelines available at www.isoiec20000certification.com.

2.4.2   Relationship scope and value/usability of the certificate

The direct benefits that service providers will experience following certification and retention of the ISO 20000 certificate are numerous. The benefits will be specific to the service provider, as each one is different in its capabilities. The direct value to the service provider of ISO 20000 certification will be articulated through the gaps identified during the capability assessment, and these are the opportunities for improvement.

In addition, there are a number of indirect benefits that could be realized:
- **Improved staff morale:**
  - Certification to the standard brings with it a new continual service improvement impetus that must be maintained in order to retain certification. The environment in which staff work will not stagnate over time.

- The standard requires the service provider to focus on its people as part of the competence, awareness and training of individuals. By investing time in identifying and, where possible, aligning role skill competencies to individuals, staff will be better prepared to conduct their daily jobs.
- The basic fact that the senior management team must work to help to achieve and retain certification to the standard is also a positive message that is well received by staff. This promotes the 'we're all in this together' philosophy.

- **Marketing** - ISO 20000 certification is a significant milestone for service providers and it is understandable that they would want to tell the world about it. This can act as a morale booster for staff, linking back to the first point here, but can also help to differentiate the service provider from its competitors. Internal service providers should not consider themselves outside of the commercial competitor space, as there will be many commercial (external) service providers who may wish to take their business away as part of an outsourcing deal.

- **Outsourcing** - Certification can contribute to an internal service provider retaining its status, as they have been recognized by an external Registered Certification Body to be doing a good job. This can also occasionally work against them, as there is a well known outsourcing mantra, 'don't outsource your problems, you should only outsource something that is working well'. However, the probability of outsourcing will be increased for a service provider who does not have certification.

- **Invitation to Tender (ITT) / Request for Proposal (RfP)** - For commercial (external) service providers, the ability to differentiate from their competitors is a key facet in their response to ITTs/RfPs. By having ISO 20000 certification, it shows that the service provider has the capability to deliver a service that is aligned to the customer needs, is integrated and is continually improving, all factors that would be well received by a prospective client. There is a health warning though: the scope of the certification may be for a management system that will not be used or may require significant re-work to support the new business. It is therefore very important that any customers validate what they are going to get, and that the service provider understands the challenges that they may face to integrate the new services into an existing management system.

As regards marketing, the main advantage **EDS** hoped to gain with certification, was to be an early adopter of the standard and thus contributing to its reputation as a company taking the lead in new developments in the field of quality.

EDS was not very well known in the Netherlands at the time, so the 'free' publicity that certification would generate was another reason to achieve certification.

Moreover, EDS Global was increasingly reporting on ITSM standard developments. "We thought it would be good to try to lead the way within EDS as well."

2.5   Assessment: how 'certifiable' is the organization?

2.5.1   Reference to methods already established

Service providers rarely start from a greenfield operation; other standards and frameworks may have been implemented prior to ISO 20000, such as:

- **CobiT™** - ISACA's Control Objectives for Information and related Technology
- **ITIL®** - OGC's IT Infrastructure Library

Firstly, the good news is that ISO 20000 is framework neutral. There is no control, either expressed or implied either way, from the standard or from either of the frameworks listed above. However, these frameworks may help towards certification to the standard if they have been implemented well; indeed, if a service provider has its own best practice way of doing things, then this is equally acceptable.

Secondly, ISO 20000 stands alone as a standard for IT Service Management, embracing all of the priority requirements to which all service providers should aspire. It provides a coherent baseline from which to develop further benefits.

It does have a relationship with other standards which partly overlap, for example:

- **ISO 9001** - quality management - overlapping primarily in ISO 20000's
  - 'Requirements for a Management System' Section 3 and
  - 'Planning and Implementing Service Management' Section 4
- **ISO 27001** - information security- overlapping primarily in ISO 20000's
  - 'Information Security Management' Section 6.6

This overlap is actually a benefit, as it supports an integrated approach to management system development and refinement. The common elements can be encapsulated within a small number of headings (see Figure 2.6).

PAS 99:2006 'Specification of common management system requirements as a framework for integration' provides a comprehensive cross-reference between the following standards, in context, to enable an integrated management system to be defined:

- **ISO 9001** - quality management
- **ISO 14001** - environmental management
- **OHSAS 18001** - occupational health and safety
- **ISO 20000** - IT Service Management
- **ISO 27001** - information security

The ISO 20000 common elements can be predominantly found in the following sections:

- **Section 3** - requirements for a management system
- **Section 4** - planning and implementing Service Management
- **Section 5** - planning and implementing new or changed services

In conclusion, if a service provider has certification to other standards, and the scope of certification is the same or wider than the ISO 20000, then the service provider will be in an advanced position to achieve and retain ISO 20000. This will, however, not preclude the

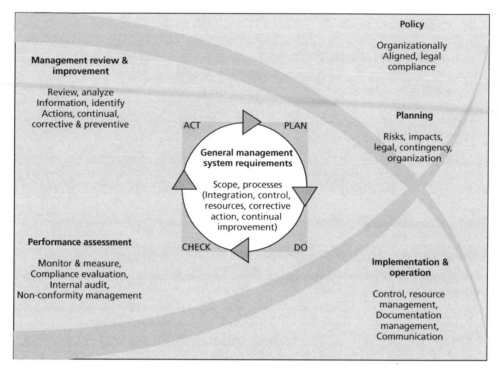

Figure 2.6   Common management system requirements

service provider from providing satisfactory evidence to the auditor that the requirements for ISO 20000 have been fulfilled.

2.5.2   Determine gaps

A structured approach to achieving and retaining ISO 20000 certification should be made, ideally using a project-based approach, as initially described in Section 2.1.3. The initial focus should be on understanding the current capabilities of the service provider within the context of the standard. The 'baseline capability' stages in Figure 2.7 provide a six stage approach for doing this.

Stage 1 - Awareness

Objective: to define the boundaries for the program and communicate the approach

This stage is primarily concerned with the service provider understanding its drivers for ISO 20000 certification, as these can greatly influence the approach and methods used to achieve and retain the certificate.

The scope of certification will need to be defined, to identify the boundaries for auditing. A scoping statement will need to be drafted at this stage and later validated by the Registered Certification Body/a registered audit company. Service providers also need to understand what

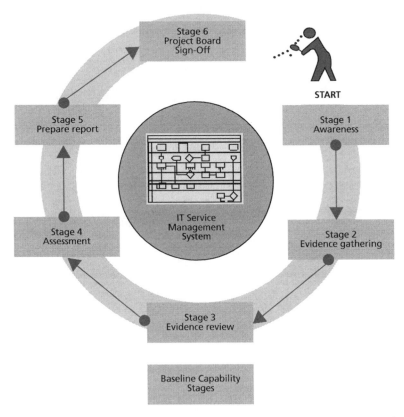

Figure 2.7   the 'Baseline Capability' Stages (within context of the overall program)

the potential impact of an ISO 20000 certification will be in terms of:
- benefits
- costs
- timescales

As previously explained, the specifics for the service provider cannot be known until after a capability assessment (Stage 4 of this process); however, generic elements can be explained within the context of the service provider's business. Examples may be drawn from the case studies available in this publication.

Stage 2 - Evidence gathering

Objective: to locate and categorize the existing evidence to enable a review to be made

One of the main challenges for most service providers is locating the current version of supporting evidence. Quite often evidence is scattered across multiple logistical and physical storage areas, with no supporting catalogue; this in itself would cause a non conformity against ISO 20000.

Therefore, this stage should address these issues by cataloguing the evidence, the DNA of the management system and making it available to the key stakeholders in IT Service Management, their staff and key touchpoints, where appropriate. This will provide an invaluable input into the review and assessment stages. It is highly unlikely that the service provider will be able to provide all evidence to support certification against the standard, as there are normally gaps that need to be addressed. For many service providers IT Service Management tools will also provide an excellent source of evidence, as they may provide, for example, history records for incidents and technology assessments for capacity management.

> Fujitsu FIP's approach to gathering the evidence was to ensure that there were documented owners for each type of evidence. For example, for data on the customers of each service, documents and records are supervised by customer managers. They manage the service implementation status for each customer in an integrated manner. These include:
> 1. progress against QMS/ISMS targets and measures taken if not yet achieved
> 2. status of revision and rectification for issues indicated in internal auditing or external audits
> 3. initiatives related to customer satisfaction
> 4. implementation of disaster and safety measures
> 5. initiatives for customer processes with frequent incidence of trouble

Stage 3 - Evidence review

> **Objective:** to review the available evidence in preparation for an assessment

Prior to conducting an assessment, there should be an analysis of the documents and records, so that an early opinion can be formed regarding conformity to the standard. The opinion will not be validated until after the assessment; however, this preparation allows focused questions to be asked of the relevant members of the service provider's staff, thus reducing the time that the staff will need to spend away from their day jobs, and increasing the knowledge of the interviewer.

Stage 4 - Assessment

> **Objective:** to determine the level of conformance to the standard via interviews and observation

An assessment should be made based upon the evidence provided to date, complemented by interviews with the process owners, managers and staff. During the interview stage, the interviewer should support the people they are talking to with constructive advice. Fundamentally though, the emphasis is on the service provider to supply tangible evidence.

Interviews do not tell the whole story though, so these need to be accompanied by observational assessment. The interviewer may ask to attend a Change Advisory Board (CAB) meeting, if they are in place, to see how changes are processed in practice; these sessions can be quite enlightening.

The service provider needs to be able to answer the following questions in context of each of the ISO 20000 requirements:

- Is the evidence **D**ocumented?
- Is the evidence **C**ommunicated appropriately?
- Is the evidence being **U**sed?
- Is the evidence being **R**eviewed for being fit for purpose?
- Is the evidence being **I**mproved where required?

This is known as the '**DCURI**' cycle of assessment.

The interviewer should discuss their findings at the end of the interview session, so that no surprises are encountered by either party further down the line.

Stage 5 - Prepare report

Objective: to produce a report detailing the level of conformance and areas requiring focus

The report will detail the findings of the assessment and should be circulated to the interviewees prior to reviewing with the senior IT management team. The reason for this is so that they have a chance to validate the final wording being used, this should be a quick exercise as they will have already checked the draft findings in the previous stage.

Obviously, the content of the report can vary; however, the following table of contents provides an insight into a well structured report:

- **introduction**:
  - business drivers for certification
  - constraints (time, cost and resource)
  - assessment approach taken (dates, interviewees, assessment method)
- **general recommendations** - institutionalize changes and emphasis on continual service improvement/review
- **conformant areas**:
  - for each requirement from Part 1 of the standard, detail the evidence seen to demonstrate compliance (in order for the service provider to continue doing good things)
  - any observations or areas of concern should also be identified (including those that could develop in to non conformant areas if left unchecked)
- **non conformant areas** - for each Part 1 requirement, confirm what the issue is regarding the non compliance, and detail options to address the situation
- **general ITSM best practice considerations** - during the ISO 20000 assessment, areas for improvement could be identified (which fall outside of the Part 1 requirements of the standard, but are ITSM best practice recommendations based upon guidance documented in the Part 2 Code of Practice and relevant frameworks such as CobiT® and ITIL®)

Additionally, the report could be enhanced further by including project-based information:

- project plan to address the non conformant areas and conformant observations or areas of concern
- document risks, assumptions, issues and dependencies (RAID)
- quality gates or review cycles

The report should be circulated to the senior management team, prior to a review meeting, to enable them to familiarize themselves with the salient points of the report.

Only at this stage can the following frequently-asked questions be answered, as they all depend upon understanding the current capability position for the service provider in focus:
- What are the benefits to the service provider?
- What are the costs (and savings) to the service provider?
- What are the likely timescales for certification?

To aid understanding of the capability status, a graph similar to that shown in Figure 2.8 should be produced. The graph shows the sections of the standard on the 'x-axis' and the number of requirements on the 'y-axis' for each of those sections. The bottom point signifies the baseline conformance to the standard, the blue bars represent the remaining gaps and the top point signifies that the section is conformant to the standard and is the target. For example, section 5 of the standard, planning and implementing new or changed services has 16 requirements, of which the service provider is conformant to 2 and there are 14 requirements left to satisfy.

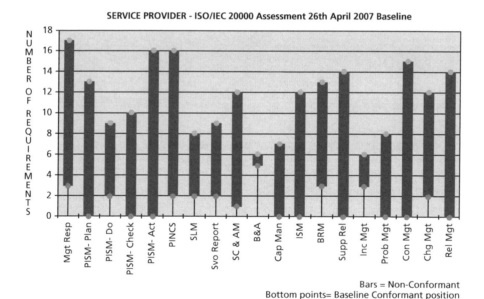

Figure 2.8   Capability assessment report

Stage 6 - Project board sign-off

Objective: to provide sign-off to proceed in to the 'certification and retention' stages

This stage is a critical sign-off milestone that needs to be satisfied prior to proceeding with the certification program, and the inevitable benefits that it will bring. Considerations for the project board of an internal or external service provider will include:

- Does the business case support proceeding?
- For external service providers specifically, can any contractual requirements for certification be satisfied within the constraints agreed?
- Is the program suitably resourced from a skills, experience and numbers perspective?
- Does the scope of certification need to be adjusted to maintain the original focus defined at the initiation of the 'Baseline Capability' stages?

Particular answers to one or more of these questions may override a negative answer to one of the others. For example, if a signed contract between a customer and their external service provider requires them to become certified to the standard within a particular timeframe, then little emphasis is going to be placed on the other questions, although they will have a role to play.

The project board should give approval to move forward to the 'certification and retention' stages if they are satisfied that the acceptance criteria at this stage have been adequately addressed (see Figure 2.9).

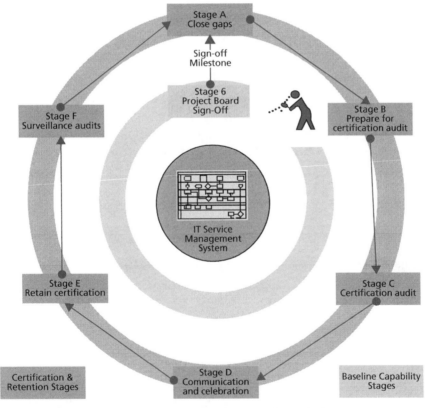

Figure 2.9 Sign-off milestone to enter the 'certification and retention' stages

2.6   Set up business case

2.6.1   Determine stakeholders

In order to understand what the benefits of ISO 20000 certification will bring to a service provider, they need to understand their current capability against the standard.

By understanding the service provider's current capability they will be able to identify those tangible characteristics and actions that will be necessary to meet the requirements of the standard. But remember, achievement of the standard should be seen as a side effect of providing a Service Management capability to a minimum set of requirements. ISO 20000 records common sense Service Management requirements. Charts provide a useful indication of the capability status; however, a detailed report is also required, recording the conformant areas (and the reasons why), the non-conformant areas (and the reasons why), in addition to any areas of concern. This will provide key input into the business case. From this information a Service Improvement Program can be defined and the Return On Investment (ROI) calculated.

The key stakeholders, and their interest in the ISO 20000 program, can be depicted in a simple stakeholder matrix, see Table 2.1; the matrix will be developed further later on in this chapter.

Stakeholder group	Perceived benefits
Customers	• speed to market of new products improved • more stable business services
Executive	• improved management information • differentiator from competitors leading to generate, retain or increase business (especially for an External Service Provider)
Service provider staff	• consistent and predictable management system • improved alignment to agreed customer requirements • staff morale improved
Suppliers	• Clearer process touchpoints with their customer (the service provider)

Table 2.1   Simple stakeholder matrix

2.6.2   Operational benefits

ISO 20000 certification will lead to improvements in the day-to-day operational management of IT Service Management in a number of ways, including:
- the efficiency and effectiveness of the ITSM management system
- maturity and penetration of the ITSM management system
- improved staff morale, leading to enhanced performance of the processes
- improved relationships with customers and suppliers

For example, **Marval** have greater insight into the effects of incidents as a result of their ISO 20000 certification. They found that they were not addressing the cumulative nature of incidents when assessing continual service improvement opportunities; they were able to address this gap and focus their efforts where pain was actually being felt the most.

2.6.3   Management benefits

A key element of the standard is the ability of the service provider to understand their current performance, and put corrective action in place to address any shortfalls against pre-defined expectations, whilst also seeking continual service improvement.

Service providers who align to the requirements of the standard will have clearer management information regarding their service performance. There will be clear key performance indicators set with measurable targets, which can be tied back to the critical success factors of the business.

Significant costs can be saved, allowing management teams to be able to realize the savings, or re-invest it into new channels.

> **Fujitsu FIP** were able to realize approximately $170,000 annualized savings by improving just one of their processes.

The top/executive management team will also benefit from a more pro-active management system. This enables them to plan ahead with improved confidence as regards their budgetary and resource requirements.

> **Nippon** reported that there was a marked improvement in their speed to respond to the business due to improved co-operation between Nippon divisions. As a result, customer satisfaction increased through developing a strong partnership with their customers.

2.6.4   Business benefits

Customers will find that their service providers are more aligned to the needs of the business. The standard requires service providers to align to the agreed requirements of the customer, and that this permeates through the service provider.

> As an example, **Nippon** found that, as a result of ISO 20000 certification, the expectation gap between the services being provided and those required by the customer was falling, which resulted in them enjoying a considerable improvement of 20% in customer satisfaction for Service Level Agreement performance. They also reaped the benefit in their IT staff becoming more service-focused, which resulted in a 300% improvement in customer satisfaction in this area.

2.6.5   Costs of not implementing ISO 20000

Quite often the costs of not achieving certification are ignored. As the awareness of the standard grows within the industry, it is becoming increasingly important to at least consider certification to ISO 20000.

For example, there has yet to be a service provider who has zero gaps when assessed against the requirements of the standard. Therefore all, or at least most, service providers will benefit from the certification. As more and more service providers achieve this, the costs of not achieving certification will be far-reaching, as customers wonder why their service provider is being left out in the cold.

2.7   Decision-making (start)

2.7.1   Decision-making on the project
Roles and responsibilities within the project, to achieve and then retain certification, need to be clearly attributed, so that activities do not fall between two roles.

The RACI-VS model is a useful technique to assist with the planning process and decision-making process. The RACI-VS model is divided into six contributory responsibility types, that can be assigned to different roles in the project. The definition of the types are as follows:
- **R**esponsible - this includes the resources who are assigned to perform a particular task
- **A**ccountable - this includes the resource who assures quality and the achievement of the process objectives; there can only be one resource assigned to this type of action
- **C**onsulted - this includes the resources who provide a stakeholder input to the certification project; it is critical that there is two-way communication between them and the management system design team
- **I**nformed - this includes the resources who are kept informed of the latest progress of the project
- **V**erifies - this includes the resources who check whether or not the products meet the acceptance criteria laid down in the product specifications
- **S**igns off - this includes the resources who approve the products following verification, and authorize the product sign off

For example, the production of a process model for change management may be assigned as follows:
- **R**esponsible - The design team is allocated to develop the process.
- **A**ccountable - The process owner is allocated to ensure that the change management process is completed as required.
- **C**onsulted - As a minimum, the configuration, release and planning and implementing new or changed service process owners must be consulted, as these processes are very closely related.
- **I**nformed - The project board will need to be kept up-to-date of progress related to the development of the change management process.
- **V**erifies - The service design authority will validate that the process achieves definition and has achieved its mandatory go/no go criteria.
- **S**igns off - The service design authority and customer representative signs off the process to confirm that it is fit for purpose.

In summary, the RACI-VS model will assist in identifying the key roles and responsibilities within the project, ensuring that approval of the project deliverables is clearly set with defined acceptance criteria.

2.7.2   Confirm the scope
Following the initiation of the ISO 20000 implementation project, the scope of certification needs to be confirmed. The draft scope defined by the service provider must be validated to ensure that it is applicable, or in other words, eligible for certification.

There are two primary options for this: firstly an ISO 20000 experienced consultancy company will be able to assist the service provider to finalize their scoping statement, or secondly, a Registered Certification Body audit company will be formally able to confirm the eligibility.

Confirmation of scope is a fundamental element of the certification process, as it defines what will be audited to validate that the management system is conforming to the ISO 20000 requirements.

2.7.3 Budgeting
Funding should be made in two stages. Initially funding is required to enable an assessment of the service provider's capability against the standard. The assessment will enable the service provider to gauge how much effort and funding will be required to complete the journey to certification, and then on-going to retention.

Subsequently, the funding identified by the capability assessment will need to be approved and allocated to the project. This funding is normally attributable to the one-off costs that will enable certification, and then the operational expenditure that will lead to retention.

Of course, these costs will be mitigated, and typically exceeded, by the benefits that ISO 20000 certification brings.

2.8   Planning

2.8.1   Set up a project team
The project team needs to be established based upon the skill requirements identified during the baseline capability assessment stages. The level of full-time to part-time commitment of project team members will be dependent upon how aggressive the project board wishes to be when attempting to be certified to the standard.

Generally, it is recommended that a full-time project manager is assigned to manage the project from initiation through to the early life of operation post-certification.

2.8.2   The 'how to' plan
Implementing ISO 20000 will always include more than reading a book and starting to implement it. It should be remembered that each published approach, be it ITIL® or CobiT® for example, are endorsed as best practice. That said, the 'one size fits all' approach is inherently risky, as culture, size, willingness, adaptability, perceived benefit versus tangible benefit, and more importantly, the people, are the variables when embarking upon managed change.

Planning needs to embrace the ethos of 'if it's not in the plan then it does not get done'. The plan needs to address the certification and retention stages identified in Figure 2.10, from A through to F and beyond.

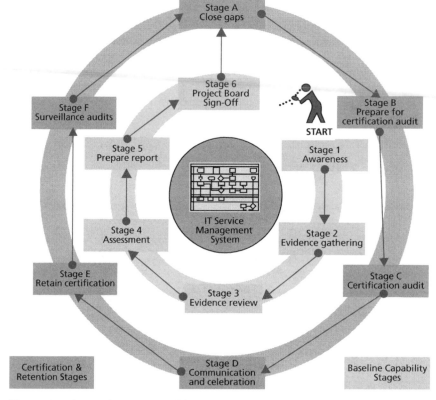

Figure 2.10   A staged approach to ISO 20000 certification and retention

The inner circle, baseline capability stages, were discussed earlier, in Section 2.5.2: 'Determine gaps'. That section describes the project go/no go gate between stage 6 of the project board sign-off and stage A of the outer circle, 'Close gaps'.

In order to assist the planning process, the stakeholder matrix can be expanded further to provide more detailed analysis. An expanded 'Stakeholder Analysis Matrix' is provided in Table 2.2.

The matrix has been expanded to include the headline changes needed to enable certification, and the perceived resistance to that change. The level of commitment refers to the stakeholder's commitment to effect the change. 'C' represents the current position of the stakeholder, and 'R' the target required state to assist with ISO 20000 certification. This provides an indication of how easy it will be to effect the change.

Obtaining certification is a great achievement, but retaining the certificate can be even more demanding. It is far too easy to focus solely upon the initial achievement of the certificate, rather than looking at how it will be retained in perpetuity. An interesting parallel could be drawn with project delivery, where emphasis is placed on delivering something into a production/live environment without due consideration of the operational requirements. It should be ensured

Stakeholder group	Perceived benefits	Changes needed	Perceived resistance	Level of commitment				
				Against	None	Let it happen	Help it happen	Make it happen
Customers	• Speed to market of new products improved • More stable business services	More open with sharing business plans with the IT service provider	May be high as this may be perceived to be sensitive information			C		R
Executive	Improved management information (MI)	Consolidate IT MI report in to Balanced Scorecard	None				C	R
Service provider staff	• Consistent and predictable management system • Improved alignment to agreed customer requirements • Staff morale improved	• Implement process improvement • Support and Train managers on cultural change • Enhance communication	• 'Seen it before' philosophy • Resources are already over-stretched, leaving no time			C		R
Suppliers	Clearer process touchpoints with their customer (the service provider)	• Implement process improvement • Enhance communication	No service culture with key suppliers	C			R	
C = Current Position; R = Required Position of stakeholder								

Table 2.2   Expanded stakeholder matrix

that continual service improvement and an emphasis on 'keeping the management system conformant to the standard' is made; hence the potential need for cultural change.

The major activities and milestones of an ISO 20000 certification plan include:
• understand ISO 20000 and what's involved
• adopt an RCB and where necessary experienced external consultancy
• determine an appropriate scope for ISO 20000
• confirm applicability (eligibility) for certification
• visualize and articulate what the project is determined to achieve, identifying high level business objectives
• obtain management buy-in
• sell the business case to the wider organization
• work with suppliers to bring them on-board and gain their help/commitment where relevant, in particular in relation to the supplier management requirements
• assess current capability against the standard - 'where are we now'
• articulate the target - 'where we want to be'
• determine the necessary methods, techniques and most importantly the resources - 'how we intend to get there'
• establish realistic timescales

- design targets and metrics - 'how do we know we've got there'
- design a continual improvement process - 'how do we keep going'
- implement a continual service improvement plan and make progress on improvements
- institutionalize change, ensuring that staff recognize that any changes as part of the ISO 20000 project are embraced as part of normal operation
- schedule a formal certification audit
- prepare for the formal certification audit
- manage the certification audit process
- gain certification
- arrange a celebration of the results
- retain ISO 20000 certification

2.9   Selecting a certification body

2.9.1   Accreditation in different countries

The International Accreditation Forum, Inc. (IAF) is the world association of Conformity Assessment Accreditation Bodies in the field of management systems and beyond. The purpose of IAF is to ensure that its accreditation body members only accredit competent bodies, and to establish mutual recognition arrangements. The IAF is supported by Regional Accreditation Bodies (eg European co-operation for Accreditation - EA) and National Accreditation Bodies (NABs), for example, UKAS (UK), ANSI (USA), JAB (Japan), TGA (Germany), ENAC (Spain) and RvA (the Netherlands). Registered Certification Bodies are then accredited by the NABs to perform amongst other activities certification audits. There are exceptions to this for ISO 20000, but in the interests of simplicity, this element of the story will not be discussed in further detail here. Figure 2.11 visualizes the certification scheme explained.

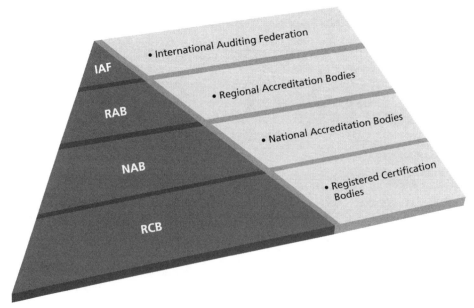

Figure 2.11   Accreditation structure

In a separate system, the itSMF UK holds the full list of RCBs for their independent certification scheme. The RCBs are permitted to operate by the itSMF UK across the globe, assuming that they meet their defined criteria.

To assist with the consistency and credibility of RCBs, the itSMF UK ensure that the RCB has at least two auditors who have passed the ISO 20000 auditor or equivalent qualification of itSMF UK. One of these auditors must be a member of the audit team assessing compliance to the standard for a service provider.

From time to time the Accreditation Bodies will validate the performance of the RCBs, to ensure adherence to the guidelines and rules.

2.9.2   Criteria for selection

Service providers looking to engage with a Registered Certification Body should firstly ensure that the RCB is accredited to audit against ISO 20000; this can be achieved by referring to the National Accreditation Body, or—for the itSMF UK scheme—to the itSMF UK's www.isoiec20000certification.com website.

Service providers typically select RCBs based upon existing relationships. For example, if service provider 'A' has used RCB 'B' for their ISO 9001 certification, it is likely that they will continue to use them for their ISO 20000 project; however, this is by no means mandatory.

> KEMA Quality B.V. was already auditing EDS Netherlands with regard to 9001, and EDS decided to select them for their ITSM standard certification as well. KEMA is a well known quality audit organization in the Netherlands, that also operates internationally. This was important, as EDS were planning to involve Belgium, Luxembourg and Scandinavia in the certification in the future.

RCBs are commercial organizations; therefore one of the other key elements will be cost. There could be a significant difference in the day rate charged by one RCB when compared to another.

If the service provider has no existing RCB relationship, or they wish to change their RCB for the ISO 20000 certification, then they should consider an Invitation to Tender (ITT) or Request for Proposal (RfP), using industry recognized processes and techniques.

Chapter 3
The certification step-by-step

This chapter explores the detail of moving from confirmation of scope through to preparing for a certification audit and celebrating success. It is complemented by the Chapter 4: 'Retaining the certificate'. This is perhaps one of the most important elements of the certification program.

The focus here is upon the early stages of the 'certification and retention cycle'; see Figure 3.1, which was first introduced as a concept during the chapter on assessment (Section 2.5.2).

3.1   Finalize scope

As discussed earlier, scoping can be a very straightforward task or a very complex task, depending upon the drivers for certification. For example, if an external service provider has been told by one of their customers that they need to achieve certification to ISO 20000 for the services that they provide to that customer, then the scope is effectively already set. However, another service provider may consider certification from an elective standpoint; the definition of the scope is therefore much more in their own hands. They may decide to reduce the scope of certification within geographic regions, functional units, customers and/or service boundaries.

Fundamentally it should be remembered that it is the management system that is being certified and not, for example, the services themselves. Scoping simply provides a capability to define against what the management system will be tested.

To formally baseline the scoping statement, which may have been set by the service provider themselves or in conjunction with external consultants, a Registered Certification Body (RCB) must be used. They are accredited by an Accreditation Body to perform certification practices, one of which is to confirm scope.

They will check that the scope:
• is unambiguous
• applies to a single legal entity

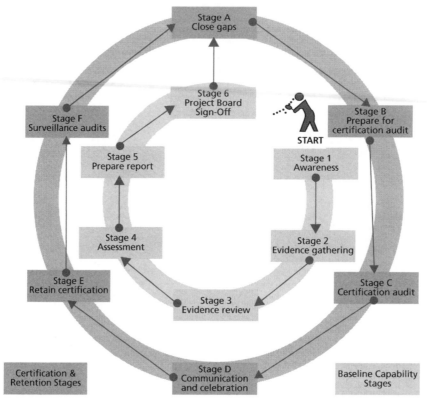

Figure 3.1   Baseline capability, certification and retention stages

- conforms ideally to the scoping statement template
- is therefore ultimately eligible for certification

3.2   Inventory of the management system

Stage B of the 'certification and retention cycle' is concerned with how the service provider should **'prepare for a certification audit'**. This is a very valuable stage in the cycle, assisting the service provider in aligning its management system to be ready for management and operation, in addition to the certification audit itself.

One of the major challenges for service providers is in understanding where their IT Service Management related documents and records are located. This may initially sound strange; however, many service providers have poor document management systems, with information replicated across numerous storage facilities and sites across the world. This issue is compounded by service providers failing to retain formal records to be used later in the ITSM lifecycle; for example, an SLA review meeting will happen, but no meeting minutes will be produced.

One of the answers to this is to develop an inventory, which is maintained and used as a single way of navigating the collateral available. The inventory will to identify gaps and maintain good document control.

This section provides examples of documents and records required by the standard. Throughout the lifecycle of a piece of evidence and its use in context, an item that started off as a document may transform into being a record; for example, a change record when initially logged could be classified as a 'document' as it shows an intention to do something; however, it also provides a 'record' that the change management process is working. Service providers should not be overly concerned about this aspect, as long as they are capable of providing evidence that they are managing and operating ITSM, in addition to simply designing and delivering it.

3.2.1 General demands

The standard is not explicit in terms of the format that documents and records are required to be held in, as each service provider will be different. It does, however provide an indication of the evidence needed, by detailing the requirement (Part 1) and providing supporting guidance (Part 2).

Section 3.1 of the standard is concerned with 'management responsibility'. It provides the foundations upon which the IT Service Management (management) system should be built. The key pieces of evidence that will be expected here include (but are not limited to) the evidence shown in Table 3.1.

3.1 - Management responsibility sample evidence	Document (D) or record (R)
Objectives	D
Policies	D
Plans	D
ITSM performance reports	R
Continual service improvement logs	R
Management Review logs	R

Table 3.1   Key pieces of evidence for management responsibility

Section 3.2 of the standard is concerned with 'documentation requirements'. The auditor will want to be convinced that there is good document management in place, including for example, version control, storage and disposal. The key pieces of evidence that will be expected here include (but are not limited to) the evidence shown in Table 3.2.

3.2 - Documentation requirements sample evidence	Document (D) or record (R)
Document management system, eg policies, functions, supporting tools	D/R
Document management process	D

Table 3.2   Key pieces of evidence for documentation requirements

Section 3.3 of the standard is concerned with 'competence, awareness and training'. Without people there would be no IT Service Management; therefore it is highly commendable that the standard focuses on this area. It does so by ensuring that staff are aware of their commitments and how they contribute to them, while being supported by their management team through appropriate training and mentoring strategies, to enable them to fulfill their roles. The key pieces of evidence that will be expected here include (but are not limited to) the evidence shown by Table 3.3.

3.3 - Competence, awareness and training sample evidence	Document (D) or record (R)
Organization chart	D
Role guides with competencies	D
Resource plan	D
Performance review schedule	D
Education/training plans	D
Performance review results	R

Table 3.3   Key pieces of evidence for competence, awareness and training

3.2.2   Working routines involved in planning and implementing Service Management

Section 4 of the standard is concerned with 'planning and implementing Service Management', the PDCA cycle. The auditor will be looking for a structured approach to establishing and continually improving the ITSM capability within the context of the service provider's plans, policies and objectives. The key pieces of evidence that will be expected here include (but are not limited to) the evidence shown by Table 3.4.

4 - Planning and implementing Service Management sample evidence	Document (D) or record (R)
Service Management plan	D
Service Management framework	D
Cost model	R
Risk log	R
Recruitment plan	D
Resource plan	D
Process KPIs	R
ITSM assessment report	R
Service performance reports	R
Internal audit plan	D
Internal audit reports	R
Internal audit procedure	D
Continual service improvement (CSI) policy	D
CSI communication records	R
CSI log	R
CSI process	D

Table 3.4   Key pieces of evidence for planning and implementing Service Management

3.2.3 Working routines involved in planning and implementing new or changed services

Section 5 of the standard is concerned with 'planning and implementing new or changed services'. The auditor will be looking to ensure that the service provider has a structured approach, perhaps project/program-based, to introducing, changing and retiring services. The key pieces of evidence that will be expected here include (but are not limited to) the evidence shown by Table 3.5.

5 - Planning and implementing new or changed services sample evidence	Document (D) or record (R)
Proposal for new or changed service	D
Associated change records	R
Implementation Plans	D
Service acceptance criteria	D
Service acceptance criteria assessment report	R
New or changed service review	R
Change management review	R

Table 3.5   Key pieces of evidence for planning and implementing new or changed services

3.2.4 Working routines involved in the service delivery processes

Section 6 of the standard is concerned with 'service delivery processes'. For the first process area, **service level management**, the auditor will expect to see strong communication between the service provider and their customers, regarding the service required. The key pieces of evidence that will be expected here include (but are not limited to) the evidence shown by Table 3.6.

6.1 - Service level management sample evidence	Document (D) or record (R)
Service level agreements	D
Service catalogue	D
Operational level agreements	D
Underpinning contracts	D
Service level management processes and procedures	D
Service level requirements	D
Service catalogue reviews	R
Service catalogue communication records	R
Change records for amendments to the SLAs	R
SLA review meeting minutes	R
Service level reports	R
Service improvement plan logs for SLM	R
Service catalogue reviews	R

Table 3.6   Key pieces of evidence for service level management

Service providers need to ensure that the information they are providing to their customers is fit for purpose. Many times service providers simply 'press the button' to print the next 'out of the box' **service report** from their toolsets, only to find that there is only a small nugget of information that the customers actually find useful. The key pieces of evidence that will be expected here include (but are not limited to) the evidence shown by Table 3.7.

6.2 - Service reporting sample evidence	Document (D) or record (R)
Service report specification	D
Customer service requirements	R
Service report catalogue	D
Service report	R

Table 3.7   Key pieces of evidence for service reporting

The auditor is also looking to ensure that customer requirements have been reflected within the **service continuity and availability** arrangements. One of the most important aspects is ensuring that the plans remain current and are assessed for impact when changes are being reviewed. The key pieces of evidence that will be expected here include (but are not limited to) the evidence shown by Table 3.8.

6.3 - Service continuity and availability management sample evidence	Document (D) or record (R)
Record of interpreting business requirements in to availability and service continuity plans	D
Availability and service continuity processes and procedures	D
Availability plans	D
Test plans demonstrating alignment to business needs	D
Service continuity plans	D
Availability and service continuity plan reviews at least annually	R
Interface between change and availability/service continuity plan impact analysis (RfC assessments)	R
Availability monitoring reports	R
Including predictive availability trend analysis reports	R
Actions from availability monitoring	R
RfCs raised as a result of availability actions	R
Test results	R
Actions from test results, continual improvement	R

Table 3.8   Key pieces of evidence for service continuity and availability management

Sound **budgeting and accounting** practices are at the forefront of many service providers minds, particularly following recent financial irregularities found with Enron and WorldCom in the USA, which had global ramifications and saw the Sarbanes-Oxley Act introduced in 2002, with facsimiles appearing around the world. The auditor within the context of ISO 20000 will look to ensure that the service provider is aligning to its own financial policies and managing any diversion from plans. The key pieces of evidence that will be expected here include (but are not limited to) the evidence shown by Table 3.9.

6.4 Budgeting and accounting sample evidence	Document (D) or record (R)
Accounting policy	D
Budgeting policy	D
Budget plan	D
Accounting reports	R
Budget reviews (future)	R

Table 3.9   Key pieces of evidence for budgeting and accounting

For **capacity management**, the auditor will be looking to ensure that there is a pro-active focus being employed with future customer plans identified and reacted to appropriately. The key pieces of evidence that will be expected here include (but are not limited to) the evidence shown by Table 3.10.

6.5 - Capacity management sample evidence	Document (D) or record (R)
Capacity plan	D
Capacity policy	D
Capacity management process and procedures	D
Business predictions and workload estimates	R
Capacity related RfC	R
Capacity reports	R
Analytical/simulation models	D
Costed options documented for satisfying customer requirements	R

Table 3.10   Key pieces of evidence for capacity management

Information security management is concerned with the auditability, accountability, availability, integrity and confidentiality of information. Service providers need to demonstrate how they are managing these five topics within and throughout their management system. The key pieces of evidence that will be expected here include (but are not limited to) the evidence shown by Table 3.11.

6.6 - Information security management sample evidence	Document (D) or record (R)
Information security policy	D
Security controls	D
Security requirements with supplier contracts	D
Security incident management procedures	D
Security risk log	R
RfCs to apply security controls	R
Security incidents	R
Security incident reports	R
Security costs	D

Table 3.11   Key pieces of evidence for information security management

3.2.5   Working routines involved in the relationship processes

Section 7 of the standard is concerned with 'relationship processes'. By now it should be clear that integration with the customer is a crucial behavioral characteristic that needs to shine through during audits. Not only does the **business relationship manager** need to be aware and respond to current and future customer requirements, but the service provider needs to react in the context of the individual's role. The key pieces of evidence that will be expected here include (but are not limited to) the evidence shown by Table 3.12.

7.2 - Business relationship management sample evidence	Document (D) or record (R)
Stakeholder and customer matrix	D
Annual service review meeting minutes	R
Interim service review meeting minutes	R
Change management records	D/R
Business requirements/plans	D
Complaints process	D
Customer satisfaction process	D
CSI log	R

Table 3.12   Key pieces of evidence for business relationship management

Having everything in place as a service provider within the boundaries of their organization is fine; however, if **suppliers**, are simply not included in the process of designing services, then issues will arise. For example, when committing to service levels, the service provider should ensure that any suppliers that will be supporting a service are able to work to the commitment levels being requested, before the agreement is signed with the customer. Equally, process touchpoints between the service provider and their suppliers should be clearly identified, to avoid conflicts further down the line. The key pieces of evidence that will be expected here include (but are not limited to) the evidence shown by Table 3.13.

7.3 Supplier management sample evidence	Document (D) or record (R)
Supplier catalogue	D
Supplier management process	D
Underpinning contracts	D
Contractual review meeting minutes	R
Change management records	D/R
Contractual disputes process	D
Supplier performance reports	R
CSI log	R

Table 3.13   Key pieces of evidence for supplier management

3.2.6   Working routines involved in the resolution processes

Section 8 of the standard is concerned with 'resolution processes'. **Incident management** is a well known process and is often associated with the service desk function. An auditor will be looking to ensure that there is control of incidents and that the customer is kept informed of any potential service level breach, so that the customer is able to plan ahead to try to accommodate the effects of the incident or at least mitigate them. The key pieces of evidence that will be expected here include (but are not limited to) the evidence shown by Table 3.14.

8.2 - Incident management sample evidence	Document (D) or record (R)
Incident management procedure	D
Incident records	R
CSI log	R

Table 3.14   Key pieces of evidence for incident management

Problem management is also a well known process, but its implementation is sadly often limited to being re-active. Encouragingly, ISO 20000 requires service providers to also include the pro-active elements of the process. The key pieces of evidence that will be expected here include (but are not limited to) the evidence shown by Table 3.15.

8.3 Problem management sample evidence	Document (D) or record (R)
Problem management procedure	D
Problem records	R
Trend reports	R
Change management records	D/R
Problem review records	R
Known error records	R
CSI log	R

Table 3.15   Key pieces of evidence for problem management

3.2.7   Working routines involved in the control processes
Section 9 of the standard is concerned with 'control processes'. The phrase, '**configuration management** sits at the heart of Service Management' is perhaps an overly used concept, but it still rings true. Service providers find it the most difficult concept to be applied. The standard does not require service providers to manage all possible types of configuration items, as this would be almost impossible. It seeks to establish that they have clearly identified a worthwhile scope, normally in the configuration policy, to which they can demonstrate alignment. The key pieces of evidence that will be expected here include (but are not limited to) the evidence shown by Table 3.16.

Change management is the primary vehicle by which the configuration information should be kept up-to-date. It is also a prime contributor to incidents, either through the lack of a change management process, or the avoidance of applying the process for whatever reason. The auditor will be looking to see if the service provider is in control of its changes, and that it is managing them through their lifecycle. The key pieces of evidence that will be expected here include (but are not limited to) the evidence shown by Table 3.17.

9.1 - Configuration management sample evidence	Document (D) or record (R)
Configuration management plan	D
Change management plan	D
Configuration management procedure	D
Configuration management policy	D
Status accounting reports	R
Change management records	D/R
Definitive Hardware Store	R
Definitive Software Library	R
Configuration audit reports	R

Table 3.16   Key pieces of evidence for configuration management

9.2 Change management sample evidence	Document (D) or record (R)
Change management process	D
Change management records	D/R
Change management review	R
Emergency change process	D
Change Advisory Board minutes	R
Forward Schedule of Change	R
Change schedule assessment	R
Change management trend reports	R
CSI log	R

Table 3.17   Key pieces of evidence for change management

3.2.8   Working routines involved in the release process

Section 10 of the standard is concerned with the 'release process'. **Release management** should be seen to work very closely with the change, configuration and the 'planning and implementing new or changed services' processes. While release management has its own characteristics (such as communication, testing and distribution/installation), it also has a significant number of touchpoints with other processes (such as problem management for updating known error information). These touchpoints re-inforce one of the fundamental principles of 'integration'. The key pieces of evidence that will be expected here include (but are not limited to) the evidence shown by Table 3.18.

10.1 Release management sample evidence	Document (D) or record (R)
Release policy	D
Release plans	D
Release management process	D
Change management records	D/R
Known Error records	R
Problem record	R
Acceptance test environment strategy	D
Emergency release procedure	D
Release management review notes	R
Release incident reports	R

Table 3.18   Key pieces of evidence for release management

3.3   Re-adjust business case

The inventory of the management system can be used in many ways, as long as it is actively maintained and is seen as part of normal operational practices. One such use is helping to refine the business case.

By producing an inventory of the working practices, which are cross-referenced to the requirements of the standard, any gaps to it can be identified. These gaps can be articulated as tangible direct benefits that will result as part of the ISO 20000 certification program. The business case should therefore be refined to reflect a more accurate picture.

Of course, simply refining a business case is not the end of the journey. The benefits and challenges should be clearly communicated to the key stakeholders of the certification initiative, and also to the key stakeholders of the service (which will include customers, service provider staff and supplier staff). The messages will need to be focused upon the target audience, and perhaps sanitized depending upon how open the service provider wishes to be with its customers and suppliers. For example, the service provider may not wish to communicate that they are about to start doing risk assessments if their customers assume that they are already taking place.

3.4   Make service improvement plan with help of assessment

Over a period of time many situations will arise which could affect the focus of a service provider and, in particular, the design of the management system; these could include:
* mergers and acquisitions
* disasters
* changing business plans
* new products and services

A 'long horizon' planning approach is therefore unlikely to reach its end goal; see Figure 3.2. This approach is epitomized by a plan which is developed at the start of the project with one major milestone (which in this context, is initially ISO 20000 certification). Taking this approach would not be too much of an issue if the distance between starting the project and being awarded the certificate was short. However, in practice, most service providers will have plans with a 12 to 18 month duration, which exposes them to many changes over the period.

Perhaps it is therefore better to plan ahead, with an improved probability of predictability, where staff have short-term horizon milestones to achieve, and subsequently realize the benefit of their endeavors earlier; see Figure 3.3.

3.4.1   Quick improvements

During the 'baseline capability stages' a view is established of the gaps which are hindering certification. Those gaps should be qualified to identify any quick improvement opportunities, which will reap benefit for the service provider and ultimately, their customers.

A short horizon plan is more likely to gain management commitment, as it is more tangible. This is a common area where service providers fail and it is explored in Section 3.9.

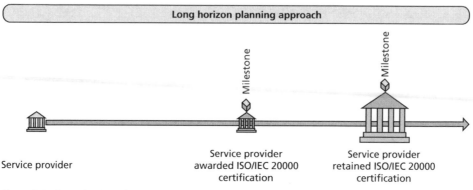

Figure 3.2   Long horizon planning approach

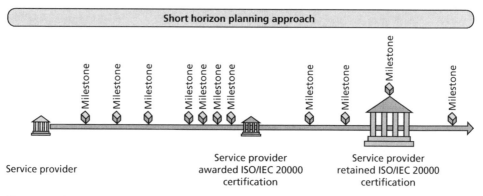

Figure 3.3   Short horizon planning approach

3.4.2   Long term improvements

It is important to note that focus should not be lost on the improvements which may take longer to implement and embed due to cultural, complexity and constraint considerations. By ensuring that the 'quick wins' are complemented by a longer term outlook, the danger of forgetting the 'big picture' and ultimate aims are mitigated.

3.5   Realize improvements

3.5.1   Check against the list of differences from the assessment

It is essential that progress against the plans and ISO 20000 certification is validated on an ongoing scheduled basis, so that:

- corrective measures can be used if the plan is compromised or at risk of being compromised
- positive communication can occur regarding progress, in order to recognize achievements and motivate staff
- interim milestones can be signed-off
- further approval to proceed can be obtained

The chart which was first introduced in Section 2.5.2, 'determine gaps' should be updated to demonstrate progress, and published to staff to encourage them to carry on their good work towards certification and then retention.

In Figure 3.4, it can be seen that the service provider has made progress in most areas; however, they have actually slipped back from their previous rating for 'Budgeting and Accounting' (B&A). This is genuinely a very real risk for service providers, as they concentrate on bridging gaps and not on keeping those areas that are working.

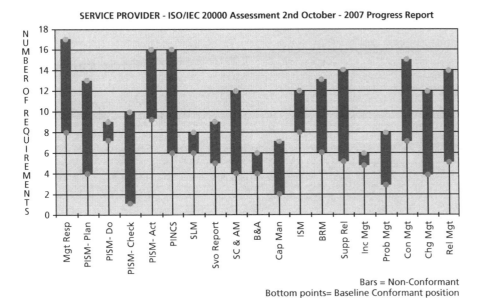

Figure 3.4   ISO 20000 Progress report chart

3.6   Internal auditing

3.6.1   Additional improvements

The standard requires service providers to perform internal audits, to ensure that they are conforming to their own Service Management plan and the requirements of the standard, thus in turn ensuring that the requirements are effectively implemented and maintained. This is in accordance to the PDCA's cycle check phase.

It could be argued that the service provider should not need to do this, as the RCB auditor will be conducting certification and surveillance audits to check this anyway, why double up on the effort? Well, Service Management operates on a 24/7 basis, and does not simply wake itself up when an RCB auditor appears on the premises every six to 12 months. Many things can change in the interim period, which demand that the service provider performs their own reviews.

The term 'internal auditing' does not imply that only internal staff can conduct an audit of the service provider's management system. They may engage with any external organization to either assist or conduct the audit on their behalf, as long as they retain management control of the process. They must take an active interest and set direction for the audit, executing any service improvement actions that the audit provides.

There are a few basic rules that need to be satisfied for the internal audit, these include:
- The auditor must be independent of the work that they are auditing.
- The auditor needs to develop an audit plan.
- The auditor must formally record and communicate their findings.

There are standards, such as ISO 17021:2006, that provide guidelines on the principles of auditing management systems, which internal auditors may find of use.

In addition to checking ongoing conformance to ISO 20000 and the needs of the Service Management plan, the internal auditor may identify best practice improvements that are outside of the scope of the standard, but which nevertheless will improve the service provider's capabilities. Other best practice opportunities may be compared against Part 2 of the standard and publicly available frameworks, such as ITIL® and CobiT®.

> **Nippon Securities** believes it is important to carry out an internal audit by specifying the target of the audit in advance, such as improving customer satisfaction.

The results of the audits must be subject to management review. The management team must take ownership and accountability of the findings of the audit, and ensure that improvement actions and their effectiveness in correcting the original issue are addressed.

3.7   External auditing

3.7.1   Preparation

If the service provider is operating to their documented management system, then there should be nothing that they need to do to prepare for the certification audit, as long as they are confident that they are ready.

In practice, there will be logistical preparation required for the RCB auditor visit; this could include:
- arranging meeting rooms
- ensuring the right people are available for the auditor
- confirming the audit schedule
- providing document type evidence for off-site review (this is normally a preference of the auditors, but not a requirement if there are security or confidentiality concerns)
- ensuring you have provided correct and actual documents
- registering what you have provided and make sure that people use these documents
- ensuring documents under change are not shown as actual, but are subject to the change process

It should be noted that the auditor will want to speak to the key stakeholders, such as the process owners and managers, plus the management team. However, their discussions will normally stretch further than this, where they will talk on an ad hoc basis to the service provider staff about the operation of their role.

The auditor would not normally wish to talk to the customers or the suppliers, as it is the service provider who is wishing to seek certification, and they must therefore be able to provide all the evidence that is required. This concept was first introduced in Section 2.2.1.

3.7.2 Execution
For '**Stage C - Certification Audit**' of the 'Certification and Retention stages' the use of an external auditor is required.

Following the agreed audit plan, the auditor will conduct their audit to a professional level, which is typically in accordance with 17021:2006 (which has superseded ISO Guide 62:1996). ISO 17021 requires a two-phase approach:
1. During the first phase, the auditor will look at the documentation of the management system and will assess the 'readiness' of the service provider. A plan for the second phase is then defined.
2. During the second phase, the implementation of the processes and the effective working of the management system is assessed. In general, there is a period of time between phase 1 and phase 2, from several days to several weeks.

Prior to leaving site, the auditor will share their draft audit findings with the service provider, so that there are no surprises and there is a final opportunity for the service provider to provide any missing evidence where applicable.

The auditor will compile their findings and produce an audit report, which will be quality checked within the auditor's company, and then issued to the service provider. If the service provider has been successful, then the RCB will award the use of a logo (see Figure 3.5 for the logo of the itSMF UK scheme) and provide a certificate. A full certification audit will occur on the third year anniversary of the certificate being awarded. This will be complemented by interim surveillance audits, which will take place every six to 12 months, and will focus on any previous areas of concern, plus a sample of processes.

Figure 3.5   The itSMF UK ISO 20000 certification scheme logo

3.8   Celebrate the result

3.8.1   Communication

'**Stage D - Communication and Celebration**' of the 'Certification and Retention stages' highlights the important stage of justifiably celebrating this major milestone. As with any type of communication, the recipient (see Figure 3.6 for examples) should be considered when producing the material; for example:

- **to customers:**
  - emphasis on external recognition of capability
  - progress made and real results in business terms
- **to service provider staff:**
  - recognize the contribution made
  - highlight internal improvements
- **to internal functions:**
  - focus upon a more integrated approach, working together, for example, the applications development function
- **to suppliers:**
  - clearer lines of communication and information flow
  - more pro-active behavior, sharing information

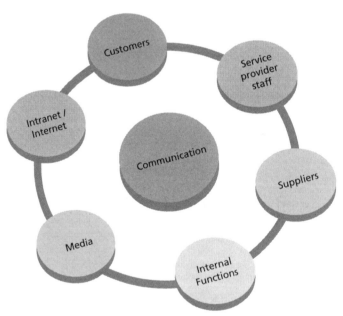

Figure 3.6   Communication targets

3.8.2   Marketing

Certified service providers may publish their certicate or the certification logo at their own websites and - if supported - at the website of their certifcation body. For the itSMF UK scheme, the certified service provider is allowed to have their organization name and scope of certification published on the website www.isoiec20000certification.com. This is not mandatory, and is at the total discretion of the service provider. In the high majority of cases service providers tend to take up this opportunity; the exceptions to this tend to be defence/security related organizations.

The service provider is also allowed to use the provided certification scheme logo on their marketing material, as long as it does not infer certification for something that is in conflict with the certification scope and applicability. For example, if the use of the logo inferred a product was certified to ISO 20000 then this would not be acceptable and it would be initially followed up by the RCB that awarded the certificate. In extreme circumstances, a certified organization can have its certificate voided for improper use.

3.9   Pitfalls and problems

There are many pitfalls and problems that a service provider could encounter during and beyond the ISO 20000 certification project; some of the common areas are described here, with thoughts on how to address them. Their impact should not be underestimated. Certification against ISO 20000 is a significant undertaking for any service provider, and these pitfalls could cause significant delays; but with careful planning, they can all be avoided or at least mitigated. The intricacies of the pitfalls, impact and possible remedial actions, will be very specific for each service provider, therefore a generic overview has been provided here.

3.9.1   Insufficient management commitment

As with all projects, including the implementation of ITIL® and COBIT® best practice, management commitment throughout the management hierarchy is vital, and without this, the project has a much greater chance of failure. When introducing, for example, ITIL® into an organization, the potential for failure may either be in part or in whole dependant upon how much of the ITIL® framework has been adapted and adopted; this is not an option when trying to achieve certification to ISO 20000, as failure to meet all the requirements of the standard will lead to a failure to achieve certification. ISO 20000 certification should not be entered into without the proper commitment, control, resources, funds and visibility. The management team may also need to ensure and promote cultural change, which will require a focus on the softer skills required to work in the new way.

One method of mitigating this pitfall is to ensure that senior management are fully informed with regards to the benefits, costs and possible problems of certification, and that there is a single team allocated to the initial certification process. This team should report progress directly to the owner of the ITSM management system.

Indicators which demonstrate management commitment are:
- senior management presentation on kickoffs and other occasions
- key quality aspects included in management goal sheet
- management reports on the project to upper management
- management calculates time for review and decision meetings

3.9.2   Poor communication

Most people understand that effective communication will help changes to be accepted and implemented. This will lead to an improved probability of realizing the benefits of the changes operationally. Good intentions at the start of a project can ultimately be compromised; communication is normally one of the first activities that suffers when the pressure is on.

Role-based communication is essential, to ensure that each role affected by any changes understands 'what's in it for me?' and 'how will I by affected?'

Depending on the size of the service provider and on available funding, it is recommended that a role is established to co-ordinate communication initiatives. This will ensure timely, consistent and effective dissemination of appropriate details regarding the progress of the project and its impact. It should be noted that the person that takes this role should not be isolated from the people who are actually making improvements to the management system, as they will provide valuable information on progress and also help to communicate the message. Reference should also be made to the additional guidelines that were provided earlier in this publication to improve the communication process.

3.9.3   Unclear drivers for gaining certification

Many service providers decide that they need to obtain certification, but they are really unclear as to why. This can lead to a great number of issues, but principally this will potentially cause problems later on down the line, when trying to prioritize ISO 20000 activities against possible conflicting business objectives. It is important to define a business case, to justify the certification and to clarify the expected business benefits associated with it. Knowledge of the drivers can also influence the way that the management system is refined.

The service provider may also find that, even though they can define a clear business case for achieving certification against the standard, it may be that they are not actually eligible, as they are not in management control of all of the processes required by the standard.

It is therefore important to understand the scoping and eligibility requirements for the certification scheme. These can be discussed with experienced consultants and RCBs; the itSMF UK website also provides some guidelines: www.isoiec20000certification.com.

3.9.4   Lack of ITSM and ISO 20000 knowledge

Insufficient knowledge of ITSM best practice could cause major problems when trying to achieve certification. Lack of understanding of basic IT Service Management could slow the process down, while service providers try to explain the principles of best practice to the relevant teams. Also, the service provider will need people with a good understanding of ITSM best practice, in order to address any potential gaps identified during the initial gap assessment. For example, the service provider will not want to (or maybe not have time to) explain to their availability manager what the contents of an availability plan should be, or justify why all changes need to approved before implementing them into an operational environment.

The people that are responsible for driving the certification process and meeting the requirements of the standard should have relevant training in ITSM best practice and in the standard itself.

In addition to this, service provider staff should be aware of the nature of the ISO 20000 project and what it will mean to them, although the key message should be 'we should be doing these things anyway, ISO 20000 certification will come as a by-product of providing a good service'.

3.9.5 One off exercise

Some service providers will consider the attainment of ISO 20000 to be a one-off exercise, which they can provide cost justification for, as it will enable them to achieve one or more marketing objectives. Unfortunately, although attainment of the standard may be quite difficult, costly and time consuming, for many service providers retaining it could be much harder if they adopt this approach.

The Registered Certification Bodies will conduct a surveillance audit (approximately every six to 12 months) of the service provider's capability; if they feel that, while the service provider was conformant at the initial certification audit, they may have failed to continue the good work, ultimately the RCB may retract certification if the service provider cannot remedy the major nonconformity within a grace period (which is normally three months). This could cause more damage in terms of marketing and image perception than not having attained certification in the first place, as the market is likely to become aware of this failure.

There are three parts to addressing this pitfall:
1. The service provider must ensure that areas of conformance are not forgotten about, while closing the gaps identified during the gap assessment; failure to do so may cause previously conformant areas to become non conformant.
2. Following certification, the service provider should ensure that the requirements of the standard are continually adhered to, in order to retain the certification; this would normally be achieved through the use of internal audits, the subject of Section 3.6.
3. There should be a strong emphasis on continual service improvement following the Plan, Do, Check, Act cycle.

3.9.6 Late start

Many service providers will underestimate the amount of effort it will take to achieve certification and the timescales associated with the various stages of certification. Leaving too much time will obviously provide maximum contingency, but may lose momentum and focus. Too little time and many of the key stages of certification could be rushed, leading to an increased risk of failing to meet audit requirements. The amount of time needed to undertake the gap assessment of current capability against the requirements of the standard will vary from service provider to service provider; these are very indicative timescales:
- **2 to 3 months (approximately)** to set up the capability and undertake the assessment (secure the team, define the approach, secure the funds, run communication and awareness programs and perform the capability assessment).
- **X months (depending on initial readiness for certification)** to close all identified gaps, which should be monitored through repeat assessments, concentrating on a natural workgroup of processes, such as configuration, change, release and planning and implementing new or changed service.
- **3 months minimum (historic audit trail)** - Registered Certification Bodies require to see sufficient evidence that processes are being adhered to; therefore they need to see a track

record. This overcomes the issue of a service provider designing a set of processes on one day and seeking certification on the next, without using the processes for any duration of time in order to prove them.

For service providers who have a fixed date to achieve certification by, perhaps as part of a contractual agreement, it is recommended that at least two months are allowed between the initial certification audit and the target date for certification. This will enable the service provider to address any areas that the auditor feels are non conformant.

3.9.7 Resource conflict

As with many improvement initiatives, it is all too easy to come up with excuses as to why the ISO 20000 activities are not completed on time, or to the required standard; one of the most common 'reasons' given is that the staff assigned to manage and close the gaps for ISO 20000 certification have split operational/day-to-day responsibilities.

Some service providers will favor short-term customer satisfaction over longer term customer and certification success. Though this is understandable and somewhat inevitable, it is short-sighted, as successful certification to ISO 20000 will ensure that the services delivered to customers will improve over time, through continual service improvement and as a result, customer satisfaction will also improve.

Service providers should ideally ensure that the resources that are assigned to the ISO 20000 certification project have little or no 'business as usual' responsibility, at least during the preparation for the initial certification audit. However, as ISO 20000 certification is not a 'one shot deal', and meeting the requirements of the standard is an on-going responsibility, it is vitally important that operational resources are included as much as possible in any relevant certification activities; they are the ones who will need to adhere to the processes and procedures which underpin the requirements of the standard, and support the retention of certification in perpetuity.

3.9.8 Resistance to change and ivory towers

The requirements of the standard may not logically fit into the service provider's current organizational model, which may make it difficult to ensure that the various requirements are being met. It may even be that the service provider does not currently have the capability required to be assessed, due to the lack of responsibility and ownership for the support of the management system.

There is also a real danger that some individuals are unwilling to buy-in to the ISO 20000 certification program, as it conflicts with their own agendas and objectives.

In order to achieve certification, service providers must be prepared to change culture, in order to effectively implement the requirements of the standard. This may include redefining the relationships with internal and external suppliers, in order to facilitate the certification process.

The following may help to change the culture:
- involving people in the design phase
- realize quick wins

- recognize people's achievements and make them visible
- show new and challenging roles to people

3.9.9   Conflict with existing initiatives

Service providers will find that they may already have existing initiatives that either conflict or complement the activities of ISO 20000 certification. This may cause problems when trying to gain commitment from all areas of the business or even from individual support areas.

As ISO 20000 is simply the certification against a minimum set of requirements and should really be a by-product of the implementation of best practice IT Service Management, service providers might easily have any number of initiatives underway, which could be perceived as duplicating some of the requirements of ISO 20000; for example, certification to ISO 27001, the information security management standard.

One possible method of avoiding this particular pitfall is to ensure that the ISO 20000 certification program is aligned with any Service Improvement Programs (SIP) that may currently exist, ensuring that all initiatives are matched against specific requirements within the standard, and that appropriate responsibility is apportioned to the owners of the initiatives, ensuring there is still a primary focus on the ISO 20000 certification program.

3.9.10 Internal and external 'suppliers'

The standard requires the service provider to have management responsibility of the processes, which includes ensuring that there is appropriate 'management control' of the external lead suppliers and sub-contracted suppliers (via agreements with lead suppliers).

A common problem exists where support agreements are already in place, and they can not be changed to effect the 'management control' requirements if needed for an agreed period of time (the service provider may also find that there are not any formal agreements in place, and suppliers will not sign up to formal agreements). This is not ideal; however, if the situation is clearly documented, a risk assessment has been performed and there are mitigating actions in place to address the risks, then this will be looked upon favorably. Equally, formal agreements with internal 'suppliers' need to be made; this can be a cultural shift for some organizations.

3.9.11 People, process and tools

ISO 20000 is not just about having the right processes in place. Section 3 of the standard refers to the competence, awareness and training of staff; people need to be developed and have clear expectations set as regards what is expected of them.

Toolsets can play a significant part in the provision of evidence as IT Service Management tools can show how incidents were categorized and assessed. Additionally, Operational Support Systems (OSS) tools, such as availability monitoring and capacity modeling tools can provide evidence of on-going management.

Service providers must ensure that there is a demonstrable evidence trail. It is not sufficient simply to have a clearly defined change management process, if it has not been communicated to the relevant people or areas, or if there is no evidence that it is being adhered to. Similarly, change records need to provide details that Requests for Change (RfCs) have been assessed for impact to the service(s) and have been approved prior to implementation.

In order to address such pitfalls, service providers must ensure that everything can be evidenced in a tangible manner. Evidence can be defined as either documents (such as policy statements, plans, procedures, service level agreements, contracts and emails) or records (such as audit reports, requests for change, incident reports and individual training records).

It is also useful to ensure that a central cross-reference library of evidence is available in preparation for the audit recording, where evidence is stored in support of each requirement. This will assist the audit process as evidence will be to hand and promote confidence in the management system. There are a number of ways that this can be achieved, from a global integrated IT process, services and operations management tool, to an extranet with links to the documents and records repositories, or the use of a structured LAN area.

Chapter 4
Retaining the certificate

'**Stage E - Retain Certificate**' of the 'Certification and Retention Stages' ensures that there is a focus on maintaining the good work that was evident when the ISO 20000 certificate was originally awarded.

4.1   Operational management

4.1.1   Maintain high levels of motivation and acceptance

Keeping the ISO 20000 certificate can be harder than being awarded the certificate in the first place. The primary reason for this is that the changes that have been made to achieve certification need to be embedded within the organizational psyche, and treated as normal day-to-day activities. Quite often, the message that is communicated to staff says: 'we are going for ISO 20000 to get a certificate'. This type of communication simply promotes the feeling within the staff base that they are just doing something to get a certificate, rather than achieving something for the overall good of the business.

The best way to maintain high levels of acceptance is to ensure that the reasons why the management system needs to change are clearly explained at a team and individual level. If one does not know why a change has occurred, then one could be forgiven for thinking it is the latest initiative and it will go away in a while. Some changes may be made to the minor detriment of an individual or team, which will benefit the service provider as a whole when the 'big picture' is brought into focus; this situation should be tackled head-on and communicated to those key stakeholders.

Human beings are individual characters helping to weave the great tapestry of life; differences should be embraced and understanding of individual needs analyzed by their line managers and process owners. Motivation can be defined as:

'the willingness to exert effort in order to achieve a desired outcome or goal which will satisfy someone's needs'

The individual must satisfy their own needs via job performance, while addressing the needs of the organization for effectiveness. One of the prime approaches that the standard addresses is that individuals understand what is required of them and how they contribute to the overall ITSM operation. This can be articulated in many ways, but a 'golden thread' from business plans through ITSM plans to the individual's own plans or aspirations needs to be drawn, so that staff can see the value of what they are doing.

According to US moon program folklore, President Kennedy once visited a NASA site and encountered a janitor. He asked the janitor, "and what's your job?" the reply was, "Mr. President, I'm helping to put a man on the moon." This demonstrates the pride that the janitor had in his job and how he saw how he contributed, in a small way, to the lunar landing. It is this concept that service providers should draw upon.

It is also important to recognize when changes are not working; there is nothing more de-motivating than a manager protecting and justifying their changes, with clear evidence in front of them that the changes are not effective. Staff can become more motivated by recognizing short-comings and doing something about it, rather than keeping their heads buried under the sand and assuming that all will become right.

4.1.2   Agreements with line- and process management

Matrix management is a regular feature of today's service providers; it brings many benefits, but sadly there are also challenges to be faced. The main challenges are conflict of direction and time prioritization. For example, in Figure 4.1, Emily Alicia's line manager is David Spencer; he manages her day-to-day time in order to help the service desk become more successful. As process owner for the Incident Management process, Stuart Wright is keen to ensure that the process is as efficient and effective as possible. The operational priorities, for example, severity 1 incidents, will take a precedent naturally over the process improvement that Stuart is focused on achieving. Therefore, the time that he could draw on to assist with process improvement from Emily and Francesca will be reduced.

Potential conflicts such as these need to be recognized and managed as the standard requires the management system processes to be subject to a plan, do, check, act cycle of improvement, and that the day-to-day operational management of the processes are working as defined.

4.1.3   Communication- and meeting structure

On-going communication regarding service performance and improvements should be made, so that the momentum can be maintained. Lack of appropriate and well communicated information is one of the main reasons for staff dissatisfaction, which will, in turn, lead to a de-motivated workforce.

Information can be disseminated through the organization structure, ensuring that appropriate information is filtered out and additional information of local interest included; some of the areas of interest are shown in Figure 4.2.

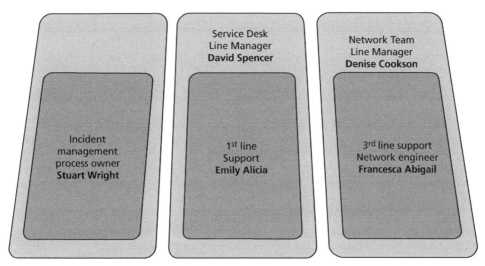

Figure 4.1   Simple matrix management table

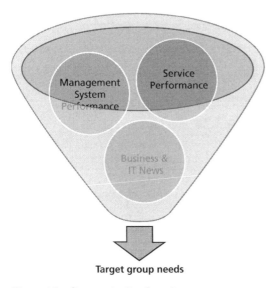

Target group needs

Figure 4.2   Communication funnel

Service providers will vary significantly in their communication strategies. A communication plan should be a common theme amongst all service providers. This should include:
- identification of key stakeholders (target groups) and granular level of communication:
  - customers
  - service provider
  - suppliers
  - external
- develop communication strategies:
  - timeliness

- select necessary information
- exclusions
• define communication methods and media:
  - internet, intranet
  - meetings
  - 1-to-1s
• develop standardized communication media:
  - templates
• establish a communication hierarchy with clear roles and responsibilities

4.2 Metrics and reports

4.2.1 Measures
Measures should be an intrinsic part of the management system. They provide a basis on which to judge how well the service provider is performing within the context of their policies, processes and business drivers. It is all too easy, however, to concentrate too much on measurements and say, 'we're achieving all of our targets, what's your problem?' when the customer says that they are unhappy. Subjective (eg customer satisfaction) as well as objective (eg percentage availability) measures should be put in place to counteract this issue.

Measures give a basis for benchmarking and assessing performance over time.

4.2.2 Measurements and metrics
When initially defining metrics it is important to have a manageable number, so that statistical information is easier to analyze. When considering the individual process metrics it is recommended that a maximum of three metrics per process are used. The metrics should be based upon qualitative and quantitative measurements.

Ultimately, the service provider's senior responsible owner will need to take an overall view of the performance of the management system; this may be through the use of a balanced scorecard. Correlation back to the service provider's and businesses' objectives is critical; so that the service provider does not become overly concerned on focusing internally, they should also focus on how well they have enabled the business to achieve its objectives.

In order to maintain the certificate, **EDS** added a dashboard to track the improvement actions that followed from the audits, in order to manage and control them in a better manner.

4.2.3 Performance versus targets
Continuing the alignment to the business theme, the critical success factors (CSFs) of the business should be driven through to the service provider, to enable them to produce a series of key performance indicators (KPIs) to confirm whether or not they are enabling the business to succeed, see Figure 4.3.

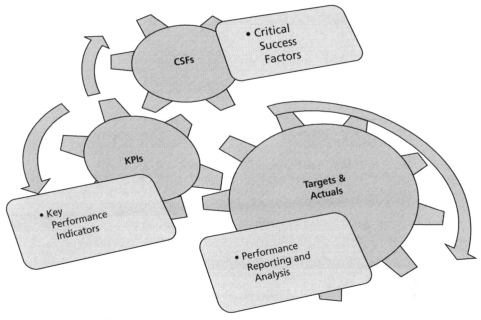

Figure 4.3   CSF to KPI relationship

Identifying CSFs allows an organization to define what is important, so that there is clear direction as a singular reference point for all staff. They should be clearly linked to the organization's strategic objectives and goals.

For example, one of 'FEDD Grand Prix's' objectives could be: 'to involve its fans more in looking at how a grand prix team is run'.

Their critical success factors could therefore include:
• fan base satisfaction increases by 25%
• merchandise revenue increases by 10%
• introduce new online services

These CSFs can be complemented by service provider KPIs; for example:
• time to introduce new services reduced by 5% (linked to merchandise revenue)
• global data centre hosting established by 2009 (linked to new online services)

This approach helps to demonstrate the 'golden thread' from business plans through to IT services, and shows how the service provider and its staff contribute to that overall objective.

4.2.4   Customer satisfaction
Customer satisfaction should be seen as a subjective measurement. For example, in the western world, as a sweeping generalization, if one was to be asked what one thought of the performance of a service over the last month, the following responses might be forthcoming:
• **asked the question early in the day on a Monday morning** - more likely to get a negative response as the working week has started again

- **asked the same question on a Friday morning** - more likely to get a positive response as the weekend is near

Human nature can be unpredictable; many things can influence how an individual feels at any one point in time; that is why the standard recommends that 'significant' deviations of customer satisfaction results should be investigated.

The standard does not require service providers to perform customer satisfaction measurements themselves; they may, for example, engage an outside agency for their expertise, as long as the service provider retains management control of the process.

4.2.5   Use of resources

Resource utilization is a formal concept that has been used in project management disciplines for many years. It is concerned with effectively using the available time of an individual resource, based upon their capability to deliver. For example, in Figure 4.4, it can be seen that Doug Ogden is over utilized, when compared to Dave Ward. This situation often happens in IT Service Management, and is normally due to scarce skills or poor planning.

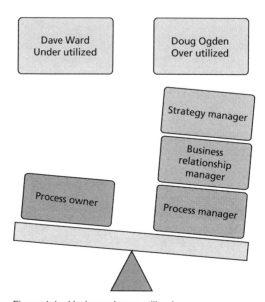

Figure 4.4   Under and over utilized resource

Service providers should try to plan ahead for the types of skills and experience that they will need to support future business plans. This should include the number of resources to fit in to the role bands.

4.2.6   Trends

Trends provide a useful indication of direction; they could be positive or negative, but the only way to know this is to understand what the target is. This ties back in to metric definition. Trends can also help to predict the future, by learning from past trends.

Stock market analysts make it their job to study equity trends, trying to identify the peaks and troughs of dealing. One lesson they have learnt is to never forget the fundamentals though: those things that can stop a trend, such as a banking system collapse.

Service providers should take notice of this, and use trends as a useful indicator of performance; but they should understand the fundamentals of why a trend is negative so that they can apply corrective action. They should also understand positive trends too, in order to repeat past successes. It is notable that in the world of Formula One, some teams are more adept at bringing positive performance from one season in to the next, as they understand the reasons why they were successful.

4.2.7   Serious shortcomings

Any major non conformities to the standard or to the service provider's own policies and processes should be rectified with due haste, based upon priorities driven by impact to the business. They should follow the normal plan, do, check, act cycle and be complemented by the change management process.

4.3   Surveillance audits

'**Stage F - Surveillance Audits**' of the 'Certification and Retention Stages' ensures that there is preparation and control for the on-going interim audits.

In addition to the initial and on-going full certification audits, surveillance audits prevail, in order to re-confirm that the service provider is continuing to perform to the requirements of the standard. A sample schedule of audits can be seen in Figure 4.5.

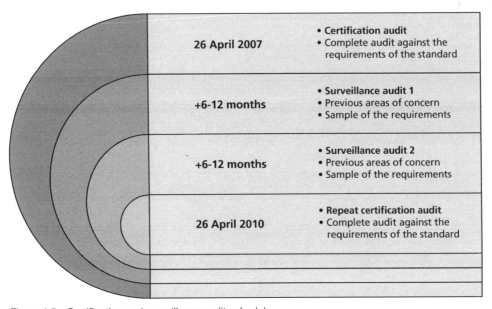

Figure 4.5   Certification and surveillance audit schedule

For a larger scale, more complex service provider, their surveillance audit frequency would be shorter and more towards the six month cycle. As is the case for certification audits, the service provider must demonstrate a track record of performance, so it is not possible to wake up the management system every six months or so and have it ready for the auditor.

If any areas are deemed to be non conformant to the requirements of the standard at a surveillance audit, the service provider is normally given a three month grace period in which to rectify the situation. If the service provider does not achieve this, or the issue is not capable of remedy in that timeframe, then the Registered Certification Body is within its rights to withdraw the certificate; at all times the certificate belongs to the RCB and is issued to the service provider while they are in conformance to the standard.

> **EDS** has both the ISO 9001 as well as the ISO 20000 certificate; the third party auditing organization executes one surveillance audit for both standards each half a year.
>
> For each surveillance audit, EDS drafts a proposal on what subjects could be audited. An interim audit takes about two days, and a fixed part to be audited each time is the Quality Management System, management and its organization. Besides this, six other subjects can be audited, being particular processes or organizational groups.

Chapter 5
Evaluate business case

5.1 Period of experience

Following the successful achievement of ISO 20000 certification, the time will come to re-visit the business case to check that the benefits are being realized. It is important that, throughout the initial stages of certification through to the on-going operation of the management system, one or more resources are assigned to effectively monitor and manage the realization of the benefits. This is quite often missed, leading to the business case almost being forgotten.

For some service providers, a return on investment (ROI) will be tangible, with a clear payback period identified; for others, a valid approach may have been to achieve certification irrespective of direct payback. Either way, the tangible and intangible benefits should be measured, based upon the original criteria that were set in the business case. Depending upon the nature of the gaps that were identified during the baseline capability assessment stages, benefits may be realized from day one of operation, even prior to formal ISO 20000 certification.

The realization of business benefits should be assessed on a two stage basis:
1. evaluation and analysis of the immediate benefits to the business following certification
2. evaluation and analysis of the benefits after a given intervening period of time in which new measures of performance are compared with previous baseline states; post certification measures may take some time to be collected and put in context, so ensuring that a prior baseline was taken, is an important part of being able to do this; this second evaluation may also lead to the use of Six Sigma or other improvement methods for further improvement gains.

5.2 Interests

The key stakeholders that were identified during the business case development process will need to be kept informed of progress against the planned realization of benefits. Any deviations to the plan, where additional benefits are realized or planned benefits lost, should be clearly identified, with supporting reasons and where possible, for the lost benefits, a corrective action plan put in place which is managed, monitored and reported on.

5.3   Operational benefits

At this stage the operational benefits identified should be clear for all to see, but they must be articulated in a way that shows the tangible improvements. For example, the following benefits may have been realized:

• a 2% reduction in incident turnaround time
• a 6% reduction in operating costs
• a 22% increase in the ability to absorb change
• a 26% increase in first line fix

5.4   Management benefits

The service provider management team should have access to useful and clear management information, regarding the performance of the management system in support of the business critical success factors. They will find it easier to correlate their performance with business success, and be able to make strategic decisions based upon future business plans.

5.5   Business benefits

Most businesses will normally see a marked improvement in responsiveness from their service providers. They may also find that they will work closer with their service providers, regarding future planning and alignment of working practices, such as IT service continuity and business continuity management.

5.6   Costs of implementation ISO 20000

After a suitable time following the award of the certificate, the final analyses of the costs of certification should be made. These should be compared against those costs identified during the business case stage, and compared against the benefits realized.

The costs of certification should come as no surprise to the service provider if they have employed good project management skills during the initial project cycle to certification. Costs would have been baselined, changes managed and tolerances set, with clear authorization limits identified.

It is important that not only the one-off costs are assessed, but that any changes to the on-going operational costs are also assessed to ensure that the complete situation is analyzed.

PART II:
ISO 20000 CERTIFICATION CASE STUDIES

Case 1:
Electronic Data Systems IT Outsourcing

CASE DETAILS	(anonymized company is allowed)
Company name	Electronic Data Systems IT Outsourcing (EDS-ITO)
Country	The Netherlands
Year and Month of certification	BS 15000 certificate issued June 2005 ISO 20000 certificate issued March 2006
Certification body	KEMA Quality B.V.
Author of the case history	**Interviewed EDS quality managers and co-authors:** Jan Boogers and Johan van Middelkoop **Interview by:** Tieneke Verheijen
Role of author	**Jan Boogers** has been an IT-auditor since 1991, and has worked for EDS since 1995, where he is assigned as the quality manager. He has been responsible for implementing ISO 20000, together with **Johan van Middelkoop**, who started working for EDS in 1997 and was assigned to a quality role in 2000. He is currently responsible for EDS' Quality Management System. **Tieneke Verheijen** is the managing editor of this ITSM Library title, on behalf of itSMF International.
Company of author	Jan Boogers and Johan van Middelkoop: EDS-ITO Tieneke Verheijen: Inform-IT
Date of case logging	October 8, 2007 October 22, 2007

All content has been taken from the interview and from other available material on the EDS ISO 20000 certification. Quotes citing directly from the interview are indicated with double quotes.

In this case description, we mention BS 15000 when it actually refers to EDS' BS 15000 certification in 2005. We use ISO 20000 when referring to actions which are still taking place and which are related to EDS' long-term ISO 20000 efforts.

If we refer EDS' measures to retain the certificate, we mean both the ISO 9001 and the ISO 20000 certificate.

1.1   Organization type

Company name	Electronic Data Systems IT Outsourcing (EDS-ITO), the Netherlands
Established	Internationally since 1962, in the Netherlands since 1980
Line of business	IT Outsourcing
Head office	EDS International B.V. Rivium Quadrant 2 2909 LC Capelle a/d IJssel P.O. Box 320 2900 AH Capelle a/d IJssel Netherlands phone: 31 181 50 22 11 fax: 31 181 50 21 99 info-nl@eds.com
Branches, branch offices	IT Outsourcing, the area being certified is infrastructure services, which is mainly situated in Spijkenisse (until mid-2008), Leeuwarden, Utrecht and Capelle aan den IJssel.
Number of Employees	1,650 in the Netherlands, of whom 750 are being employed within the scope of the certification.
Areas of specialisation	IT Outsourcing

Table 1.1   Outline information on EDS

1.1.1   Organizational size

EDS Netherlands employs nearly 1,650 people, working on client locations and in EDS offices located in Amsterdam, Capelle a/d IJssel, 's Hertogenbosch, Leeuwarden, Sittard, Spijkenisse (until mid-2008), The Hague, Utrecht and Maastricht.

As the scope of the certification focuses on "the integration, delivery and maintenance of end-to-end IT infrastructure services (Computer and Network Operations) from within the boundaries of EDS ITO Netherlands", its focal points at the time of the certification were in Spijkenisse and Leeuwarden, with some infrastructure also being situated in Utrecht and Capelle aan den IJssel. This business unit employs approximately 750 employees.

1.1.2   Main activities

EDS is a leading global technology services company delivering business solutions to its clients. Its main activity is offering information technology and business process outsourcing services to clients in manufacturing, financial services, healthcare, communications, energy, transportation, consumer and retail industries, and to governments around the world.

In the Netherlands, EDS has two main branches, being IT infrastructure services and application development and maintenance. The second branch was not included in the certification's scope.

IT services are, and always have been, EDS' core business. Therefore, well-functioning IT-services are of vital interest to the organization.

1.1.3   Customers

Due to the nature of outsourcing services, EDS serves external customers, both nationally and internationally. In the Netherlands, which is often regarded as the gateway to Europe, having the largest seaport in the world, the company shows its skills in the transportation sector. Large chemical companies also rely on EDS' services. In the telecom sector four out of five mobile operators are being served by EDS.

Among EDS' clients in the Netherlands are ABN AMRO, AEGON, DSM, the Dutch railway company and the Dutch Ministry of Transport, Public Works and Water Management.

Abroad, they provide services to organizations such as Kraft Foods and the Ministry of Defence in the United Kingdom (UK). In their tenders, these organizations specifically asked for ISO 20000 certificated providers.

1.2   Drivers for certification

The main driver to obtain BS 15000 certification was the wish to be an "early adopter" of this quality management standard for IT Service Management. Also, EDS Global was increasingly asking for process standardization, and mentioning BS 15000 in this respect.

"We already had a long history of being ISO 9001 certified (since 1993, ed.), and we had developed quite an extensive internal system to implement processes, based on ITIL. We were also monitoring customer satisfaction quite thoroughly. Therefore, we were under the impression we already met the (then still) BS 15000 requirements quite well. We thought it wouldn't be too big a leap to add BS 15000 certification to our ISO 9001 certificate."

"Another reason was that the outcomes of the ISO 9001 audits had become a bit predictable, and we needed a new challenge. Moreover, the ISO 9001 certification didn't assess the actual quality of our activities, while BS 15000 (now ISO 20000) does certify the quality of an organization's processes. As in ISO 9001-2000, process control has become an important part, besides customer satisfaction and management responsibility, becoming BS 15000 certified seemed to be a logical next step for EDS."

"As we were facing re-certification in February 2005, we consulted our auditor to see what it would take to add BS 15000 certification. We decided to start with the certification for both ISO 9001 and BS 15000, with the option of skipping BS 15000 if this turned out to be too much of a challenge. This 'pilot certification' would at least provide us with an insight into how far we actually were in meeting BS 15000's requirements."

These drivers were of a completely different nature to the main driver for the previous ISO 9001 certification. That certificate was necessary because clients were asking for it. Not getting ISO 9001 certified would have eventually resulted in fewer clients.

1.2.1   Main initiators

The main initiative was taken by the quality managers at that time, Jan Boogers and Johan van Middelkoop.

Jan Boogers had also previously managed the ISO 9001 certification. He graduated as an EDP auditor at the Dutch university of Tilburg in 1991.

After his studies of Business Administration at the Dutch Agrarische Hogeschool in Delft, Johan van Middelkoop followed a Master of Total Quality Management at the Dutch Hogeschool Zeeland and the British University of Humberside from 1994-95. He is currently studying EDP auditing at the Dutch university of Tilburg.

1.2.2   Business case
"We drafted a small overview of where we stood with ISO 9001, where we thought BS 15000 would take us, and the advantages, disadvantages and risks we thought there were. This was to gain management attention for BS 15000 certification and enable their decision-making on this subject."

1.2.2.1 Benefits
The main advantage that EDS expected to gain with certification, was to be an early adopter of the BS 15000 standard, thus contributing to its reputation as a company taking the lead in new developments in the field of quality.

EDS was not very well known in the Netherlands at the time, so the (free) publicity that certification would generate was another reason to seek accreditation.

Moreover, EDS Global was increasingly reporting on BS 15000 developments. "We thought it would be good to try to lead the way within EDS as well."

"Our auditor thought it a challenge as well to have a first customer for BS 15000 certification within the Netherlands. So, there were more advantages to more parties involved."

1.2.2.2 Costs
EDS did not quantify the costs of the certification, as quality in EDS is "part of everyone's regular job". "It is the thing you do or don't do while you are doing your job, so we didn't assign man hours to quality improvement."

Furthermore, the quality managers estimated it would not cost large amounts of extra time or money on top of the costs for the ISO 9001 implementation (which had been absolutely necessary as clients had requested it), and the costs for implementing the ITIL-based processes, as well as the costs for creating overall quality awareness within the company.

1.3   Quality management at the start of the project
As mentioned in Section 1.2, EDS was already ISO 9001 certified and knew the ITIL processes. For these reasons they decided to try to acquire the BS 15000 certification together with the ISO 9001 re-certification in February 2005.

When the company became ISO 9001 certified in 1993, a small amount of quality awareness became apparent, although quite abstractly and only related to the ISO 9001 standard. There were voluminous quality handbooks, which were mainly kept in cupboards rather than on people's desks.

1.3.1   IT Service Management methods established

In order to improve the quality awareness, the ITIL IT Service Management processes were linked to ISO 9001's quality management system in the mid-nineties. The processes, procedures and working instructions were made available online. This made the idea of quality more tangible, because people take part in processes every day.

All employees are trained in the ITIL processes, and the company also stimulates responsible staff to become a service manager or a practitioner in a particular subject.

Since 2000, the Plan-Do-Check-Act cycle has been introduced in the organization, and was quite firmly established at the time of the BS 15000 certification. Staff who issued a proposal for improvement, should also indicate how this improvement could be measured and how to act upon this measurement.

1.4   Parties involved

1.4.1   Management staff

At that time, the Management Team comprised ten group managers, of whom the most important were the managers of the Unix group, the Windows group, the Mainframe group and the manager of the Network Services group. They were directly responsible for keeping the infrastructure available.

Over the preceding six years, their interest in the subject of quality had been growing steadily. They were held responsible for meeting their SLA targets, and a traffic light dashboard had been introduced previously to show a 'red light' (insufficient) when they failed to meet their targets, so that they already had a direct interest in controlling their processes.

Moreover, the manager of EDS-ITO, region North, being the head of the Management Team, was very committed to having the first BS 15000 certification in the Netherlands and within EDS. According to Jan Boogers, this has been the most important factor to the successful acquisition of the certificate. "Without management commitment, you can (almost) forget about certification, or you should be extremely lucky".

This manager assigned accountability for achieving certification to the complete Management Team. This was done by formulating objectives on the strategic level, and transcribing these to measurable targets on the tactical and operational level. Both management and staff are assessed against these targets. This is done by means of a Balanced Scorecard (BSC), which is an integral part of the Quality Management System at EDS.

The head of the Management Team was also very involved in the preparation of the certification. In the period before the external audit in February 2005, there were teleconferences with the Management Team every two weeks, to assess where the current status of the company and to see what could be further improved. The head of the Management Team always attended these meetings and actively took part in them. Moreover, he monitored the attendance of the other managers and asked them if they needed help when they failed to attend or did not meet their schedule.

1.4.2 Employees
Staff were kept up-to-date via newsletters and by their own management, who took part in the teleconferences every two weeks. "We didn't do an awful lot of extra quality awareness training. A large amount of staff were already being trained in ITIL Foundations. This also helped to contact non-EDS people, which helped to give a different perspective on problems."

Through goals in their personal development plan, responsible staff are stimulated to acquire further ITIL certification, for example to become a service manager or a practitioner. For this reason EDS now employs quite a few service managers.

Furthermore, EDS has an interactive EDS University on the intranet, where staff can follow all kinds of education, such as on the subject of ISO. The ITIL volumes can also be consulted online.

"In order to get people involved in the subject of ISO 20000 and increase their quality awareness, we organized small workshops in which people could assess their own processes. In these workshops, we checked our own internal self-assessment findings against their own assessments."

The quality managers' role was a supporting rather than a leading one. "Only when managers of the different departments asked us to, did we organize meetings and presentations for their staff, on subjects such as ITIL, quality and teamwork."

1.4.3 Customers
There was no communication with the clients before the certification was achieved, as it was considered to be an internal matter. "Clients are mainly interested in whether the promised services are being delivered, not how they are being delivered."

After the certification, potential clients were informed of EDS' ISO 20000 certificate, in communications regarding Requests for Proposals (also see Section 1.11 on the evaluation of the business case).

1.4.4 Subcontractors
"We only discussed our plans for certification with subcontractors with whom we are directly in touch, such as the real estate company maintaining our housing. The department managing procurement was also involved, as they have also been charged with acquiring personnel, and certification requires personnel who are aware of quality and familiar with processes. For example, personnel should have an ITIL Foundations certificate. We didn't involve large providers such as Microsoft, HP, IBM and DELL."

1.5   Initial assessment

As mentioned in Section 1.4.2, EDS pursued an internal self-assessment through small self-assessment workshops. "As ISO 20000 consists of thirteen processes, we organized workshops with the persons who were most heavily involved in each of those processes, within the groups Unix, Windows, Mainframe and Network Services. Altogether, ten to twenty key people participated in the workshops."

"We had already assessed the group against the checklist (included in the BSI BS 15000 package we had bought) and discussed the results with the people who were actually involved in the process: what stage did they think they'd reached? If any discrepancy occurred between our assessment and their own assessment, we discussed this and tried to reach consensus. This was very motivating and informative for many people, who sometimes weren't even aware that we were already taking a lot of quality-related actions."

In putting together this assessment program, it was very helpful that the quality managers had knowledge of the auditing process from within, following their education and their practical experience with auditing in other fields, such as the yearly SAS 70 audits.

"The self assessment resulted in the conclusion that this wasn't very new to EDS. We were already thinking and working very much according to processes."

EDS did, however, find two opportunities for improvement:
* **turn the organization from a reactive one into a proactive one** - "We found out we could expect a more proactive attitude from people, as they were mostly reacting to problems."
* **better use trend analyses** - "It turned out that though we were measuring, we could focus more on trends and plan how to act on them."

"Though we scored sufficiently for all processes, availability management and capacity management were somewhat weak, namely in the Unix and Windows group, while the Mainframe group was far more mature due to its 'critical to business' nature. Furthermore, there are only a few tools available for availability and capacity management, so our Metrics Team had to develop them themselves. We can now measure the availability of each machine, but we are still developing tools to measure the end-to-end availability."

1.6   Decision to go for certification

From the start, the intention was to acquire BS 15000 certification alongside ISO 9001 certification. There was, however, a back-out opportunity if this turned out to be too complex. In this situation only the ISO 9001 certificate would be audited and hopefully re-issued.

1.6.1 Scope

The scope of the existing ISO 9001 certificate included:

> *The integration, delivery and maintenance of high quality IT infrastructure services for various platforms (Computer and Network Operations) from ITO Netherlands. Services include "monitoring, support and reporting".*

This scope was adjusted somewhat in order to arrive at the final scope of the BS 15000 certificate:

The IT Service Management System that covers the provision of "the integration, delivery and maintenance of end-to-end IT infrastructure services (Computer and Network Operations) from within the boundaries of EDS ITO Netherlands". This is in accordance with the EDS service catalogue and includes all IT Service Management processes and the management control of the interfaces that support them.

Application development and maintenance was not included in the scope, as clients for this discipline do not ask for ISO 20000 (or even 9001) certification in their Requests for Proposals. They are more interested in maturity models such as CMMI. As more maturity would therefore result in more added value, the application development and maintenance department decided to focus on maturity instead of the ISO quality standards.

The scope included all locations in the Netherlands which are involved in providing infrastructure services. As mentioned before, focal points are Spijkenisse and Leeuwarden, followed by Utrecht and Capelle aan den IJssel.

1.6.2   Objective
EDS-ITO wanted to become an early adopter of BS 15000, in order to take the lead on quality management standards both within EDS Global and within the Netherlands. This way, they wanted to generate (free) publicity for company brand awareness and gain an advantage in acquiring new customers.

1.6.3   Organization
The two quality managers initiated and advocated the certification track, by regularly organizing teleconferences and supporting managers by informing their staff.

For this certification, the BS 15000 standard has been integrated into the existing quality handbooks. Besides the quality management system, it describes the most critical processes such as release management, incident management, problem management, change management and asset management. The handbooks are on EDS' intranet, and almost each desk has a quick reference card for those key processes.

With the help of the auditing company, the less critical processes have been described in less detail, resulting in a quality handbook which is as manageable as possible.

1.6.4   Funding and resource plan
All EDS' employees should see quality as a regular part of their job, so no extra hours or budget have been assigned for this activity.

The quality managers also still have other duties within EDS: Jan Boogers as an internal and external security auditor and Johan van Middelkoop as the process owner of the problem management process.

Johan van Middelkoop is now primarily concerned with quality, including internal quality auditing, while Jan Boogers is focusing on "auditing in general", such as compliance and security auditing, both internally and externally. They can take over tasks from each other and replace each other as required.

1.6.5   Action and time plan
A re-assessment had been scheduled for the ISO 9001 certificate in February 2005. It was about six months before this re-assessment that the idea of combining it with a completely new BS 15000 audit was established. Therefore, the deadline and time period in which preparation could take place was very clear from the beginning. As the organization was already quite mature in quality as well as process awareness, this period was not insufficient. Together with the Management Team, workshops were developed and scheduled in this period.

1.6.6   Communication plan
Communication on quality was issued through newsletters, workshops and presentations to the different groups, for example, on ways in which to avoid scoring a "red light" in the traffic light dashboard which was already established. These results were published on the company's intranet and discussed in weekly teleconferences with the managers of all responsible groups.

1.7   Preparation for certification

1.7.1   Selection of the certification agency
KEMA Quality B.V. was already auditing the organization with regard to ISO 9001, and EDS decided to select them for their BS 15000 certification as well. KEMA is a well known quality audit organization in the Netherlands, who also operate internationally. This was important, as EDS were planning to involve Belgium, Luxembourg and Scandinavia in the certification at a later date.

"Another reason for choosing KEMA was that in the past we'd had some bad experiences with a third party audit organization who quibbled on small details. As we didn't think this useful or comfortable for the people who were being audited, we managed to reach consensus with KEMA on how auditors could provide criticism but think on and stay realistic at the same time. Luckily, since then, we've always had an auditor who didn't apply the standard as if it were a law, but who tried to find out whether people were committed to constantly improving themselves. This auditor can get along with management very well, but makes them a bit nervous at the same time, as he doesn't shy away from well-founded criticism, which is very useful."

1.7.2   Determine scope with certification agency
The scope agreed upon included:

> *The IT Service Management System that covers the provision of "The integration, delivery and maintenance of end-to-end IT infrastructure services (Computer and Network Operations) from within the boundaries of EDS ITO Netherlands". This is in accordance with the EDS service catalogue and includes all IT Service Management processes and the management control of the interfaces that support them.*

1.7.3   Collecting data on the management system

The auditor supported EDS in the preparation phase by indicating what still needed attention. Mainly, the attitude of staff needed to change, from reactive to proactive, and more trend analyses needed to be executed and used to improve the processes.

1.7.3.1 Process traffic light

For the most important processes, such as incident management, problem management and change management, EDS was already using *internal* traffic light reporting (Table 1.2).

Incident Traffic Lights By HUB - Tower - Capability - Delivery Team									
Open Incidents and Incidents Closed between DD/MM/YYYY and DD/MM/YYYY									
HUB	**Tower**	**Capability**	**Delivery team**	**Result**	**Measured total**	**Red**	**Amber**	**Green**	**No SLA**
Region				◇	**Hub total**	XXX	XXX	XXX	XXX
	Department name			◇	**Department total**	XXX	XXX	XXX	XXX
	Department name	**Capability name**		◇	**Capability total**	XXX	XXX	XXX	XXX
	Department name	Capability name	Team name/ location	◇	XXX	XXX	XXX	XXX	XXX
	Department name	Capability name	Team name/ location	–	XXX	XXX	XXX	XXX	XXX
	Department name	Capability name	Team name/ location	■	XXX	XXX	XXX	XXX	XXX
	Department name	Capability name	Team name/ location	•	XXX	XXX	XXX	XXX	XXX
	Department name	Capability name	Team name/ location	•	XXX	XXX	XXX	XXX	XXX
	Department name	Capability name	Team name/ location	◇	XXX	XXX	XXX	XXX	XXX
	Department name	Capability name	Team name/ location	•	XXX	XXX	XXX	XXX	XXX
	Department name	Capability name	Team name/ location	■	XXX	XXX	XXX	XXX	XXX

Legend:
■ RED: > 10% of measured incidents failed SLA (with at least 5 Red)
◇ AMBER: 5% or more of the total measured incidents failed SLA
• GREEN: Less than 5% failed SLA
- No measured requests in the reported period
(1) Incidents measured: all active cases registered that have received a valid SLA label
(2) No SLA: all active cases registered that have not received a valid SLA label
Note: all open and closed incidents are in the scope of this report
Report Printed on DD/MM/YYYY
Owner: Metrics Emea Requests

Table 1.2   Sample traffic light report for incident management

"This came into existence more or less spontaneously, with managers asking for more measurements of processes. It started with the incident management process, because management thought they were doing well, but clients didn't. So we tried to make this measurable by defining Key Performance Indicators (KPIs) based on their SLAs. These KPIs have been developed by the mother company in the USA and include definitions of severity-1 and 2 incidents, their required resolution time and escalation routes if they can not be solved in the time required. This evolved into very simple metrics, which were gathered in a report, and later on, a colour was added to the results. Then, suddenly, we saw messages on doors saying 'we are green!'"

"This constant visibility of groups being 'red' (insufficient performance), 'amber' (sufficient performance in danger) or 'green' (sufficient performance), stimulated everyone to proactively avoid becoming 'red'. The 'threat' alone of degrading a level turned out to be sufficient for people to start thinking about opportunities for improvement."

So, this traffic light dashboard worked particularly well to enhance quality awareness and proactivity among the staff and was then also introduced with other processes such as change management and problem management. Finally, a special "Metrics Team" was assigned with responsibility for it. The traffic light dashboard is such a success, that other EDS organizations in North and Central Europe have introduced it as well, among them Scandinavian countries, Germany, Middle and East European countries, Belgium and Luxembourg.

"People often start to measure KPIs way too ambitiously. EDS Netherlands started with a limited number of key KPIs, mostly two per process, in order to get the management used to using them. After a while, when people have quite some experience with them and they are firmly established, they start asking for additional information by themselves, in order to steer the process better. Then, variable KPIs can be added. Those can change over time, as KPIs tend to become part of people's behavior and then don't need to be measured every month anymore."

"Furthermore, management can only oversee ten to fifteen KPIs. If more KPIs are being presented to management, the 'big picture' can not be distilled anymore."

If everybody is scoring a green traffic light, attention to quality sometimes diminishes. Market developments may also lead to new objectives. That is why the target measures of the performance indicators are lifted periodically. This results in people scoring 'amber' or 'red' again, and this provokes improvement actions to meet the new targets. This way, with a few indicators the organization is growing to maturity step-by-step.

1.7.3.2 Client traffic light

Besides the *internal* dashboard for its processes, EDS also uses an *external* dashboard for client management: the *Service Excellence Dashboard*. This was a demand from EDS Global management, as they wanted to know the status of their top 80 clients. The dashboard shows its most important clients and their satisfaction on a certain amount of service aspects, indicated by the clients themselves, by EDS' *Client Delivery Executives* and measures of various performance indicators indicating EDS' performance against their service level agreements (Figure 1.1).

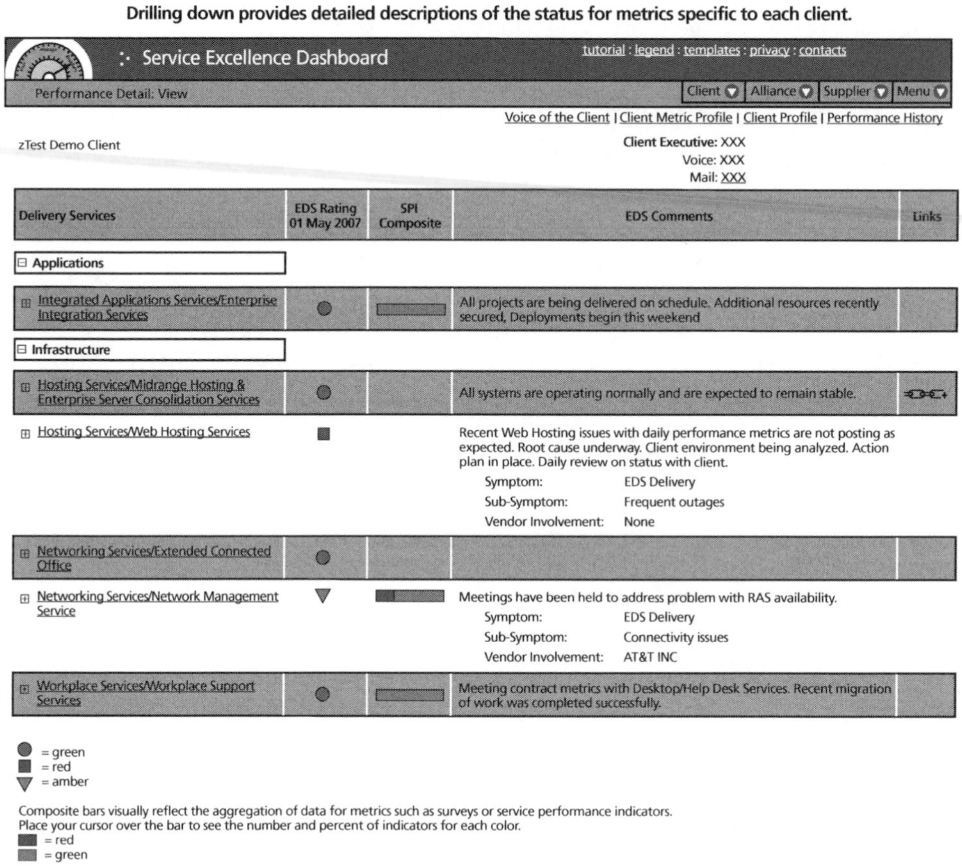

Drilling down provides detailed descriptions of the status for metrics specific to each client.

Figure 1.1   Service Excellence Dashboard

In this series, the client's own assessment comes first. "Even when the KPI's indicate EDS is meeting SLA targets, if the client is not satisfied, the light will be 'red' instead of 'green'. When this dashboard was introduced, if one of the clients indicated a red traffic light, EDS' highest executive phoned the responsible managers to check to see whether he could be of any assistance. After a few years it became a matter of daily routine for managers to check their customer's satisfaction and act upon it." Once again this shows the large amount of management commitment to quality within the company, and its impact on the success of those kinds of instruments.

The Service Excellence Dashboard is also available online for clients (Figure 1.2). They can click through on every detail that they wish to check. This provides another driver for the process managers. If a client is not satisfied with actions taken by the process owner, he has the opportunity to escalate his complaints to a higher level.

Moreover, EDS built an *internal* Contract Information System storing all service level agreements. This system pays special attention to clients who are strongly dependent on EDS' IT services. It describes why these clients are so dependent. In this way, support staff know which specific problems occur at a client's side when incidents or problems happen in these 'Key Production Environments (KPEs)'. This helps them to assess the impact of these incidents and problems.

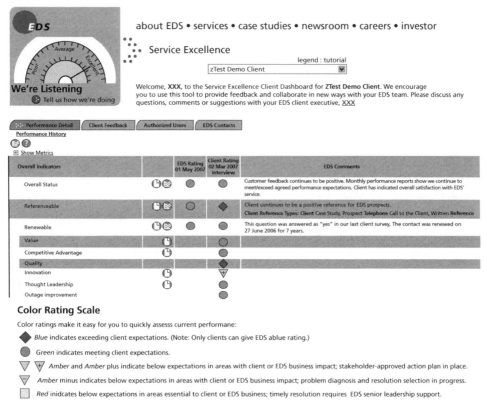

Figure 1.2   Service Excellence Dashboard 'performance detail' page for client

1.7.4   Establish service improvement plan

The traffic light dashboard proved its value in changing people's attitudes from reactive to proactive. It stimulated people to avoid becoming 'amber' or 'red', even *before* the report was published. For example, by looking at problems that actually had occurred, thinking of similar problems that *could have* occurred, and how these problems could be prevented in the future. They started investigating incidents, changes and problems by themselves and they also started to make improvement plans on their own.

"We were already demanding a Root Cause Analysis for all severity-1 incidents at that time, and we added to this requirement that not only corrective measures should be described, but preventive measures as well. We put quite a lot of effort into training large groups of people in analysing root causes. So, we have a large amount of staff who are now very capable of making Root Cause Analyses. They are behaving noticeably more proactively."

"We also introduced a conference call each Monday afternoon, discussing both the internal and the external dashboard with the capability managers and the service delivery managers. In these conferences, special attention was paid to the subjects that had been assessed with 'amber' or 'red' in the latest report." Management makes improvement plans (*going for green plans*, Table 1.3) for all points that do not score a green light, and should keep track of actual actions being taken to implement the improvement. All improvement plans and their progress are discussed weekly.

Account/dashboard client name	XYZ Project/Account		
Action plan type	Client Interview		
If other, describe			
EDS rating of overall status	Amber		
Client rating of overall status	Amber		
EDS rating of non-green service offering	Amber		
Service offering name	Application Development and Support		
		Solution center	ZXY SC
Go for green date	DD/MM/YYYY	Current date	DD/MM/YYYY
Go for amber +	DD/MM/YYYY	Client executive (CE)	Joe Smith, Phone: XXX
Go for amber	DD/MM/YYYY	Client delivery executive (CDE)	Lori Marks, Phone: XXX
Go for amber –	N/A	Program manager	Mark Johnson, Phone: XXX
Start red on	N/A	Go for green plan's approved date	Not approved yet

Project name/description	Project XYZ Analysis phase
Issue Number	1
Issues/Problems	List the issues that need to be addressed or the problems that need to be resolved in order for the project to return to GREEN status.
	EXAMPLE: The project scope did not have a formal signature from the client. The scope increase is 20% and this needs to be negotiated with the client.
Actions	List the EDS actions required to address the issues/problems. Actions can be levelled, for example:
	Step 1: reduce scope of project and revise plan to meet schedule Action A: review scope for opportunity to reduce to meet schedule Action B: prepare revised project plan Action C: receive client approval of project plan Action D: EDS resource to plan
	Step 2: Deliver to revised plan Action A: successful initial implementation
Action owner	Responsible party for completion of the action. (EDS or Client)
Start date	List the start date for all actions.
Baseline completion date	List the baseline completion date for all actions.
Current completion date	List the current estimated completion date for all actions.
Project date slippage	Days behind schedule and criticality due to date slippage. 0 to 1 week - Amber Beyond 1 week - Red
Special resource needs	List any additional resources required to return the project to GREEN status.
Status	List the status of the action items: not started; in progress; on hold; complete.
Issues/obstacles/ comments	List the issues/obstacles/comments for each action items that are not in Complete Status and could impact the execution of this plan.

Criteria to move from Red to Amber - on planned target date	
Issue Number	1
Action/step to be completed to meet target	Action C: receive client approval of project plan
Current status	Complete
Action owner	

Table 1.3   Going for green action plan template

Furthermore, in order to be able to discover trends and act upon them, EDS started to store data gained from process measurements. Before the Monday afternoon conference call, people are provided with a report stating the most important trends on incident, problem and change management, indicating if quality is increasing or decreasing. The Metrics Team also provides the context of these metrics, indicating whether trends are positive or negative.

1.8   Internal audit

To achieve certification, and to retain the certificate, both ISO 9001 and ISO 20000 require an internal audit program, in order to check whether planned and implemented improvements are delivering the expected results.

The EDS quality managers plan those internal quality audits in the same way as the external audits are planned, making sure that all processes are audited at least once every three years, the period after which an organization has to be re-certified.

"As this is quite hard to manage with only two internal quality auditors, we try to find people who can co-operate in auditing processes. That's why we ask the process owners to deliver a written audit report on their processes, after we've provided them with audit guidance such as procedures, schedules and checklists with default questions for each process. This checklist has been composed of questions from the BS 15000 checklist, and criteria which we find important ourselves, such as how to fill in a change record."

"On the other hand, we try to stop the large number of audits from driving our people crazy. Besides the ISO 20000 external surveillance audits every six months, a SAS 70 audit is executed every year. At these audits, processes like incident and change management are assessed as well, and we also see this as an internal quality audit, which we will not do all over again. So, we distinguish default (external) audits that are already being executed, the process audits with checklists by the process owners and the more complex audits, which are being executed by the internal quality auditors."

The audit report resulting from the internal audits is discussed with the people involved, and the findings from the final version are gathered on an internal quality improvement list. This list defines the results, the risk for the company's business, the corrective measure, who is going to implement this measure, and when it has to be finished. This list and the progress of the improvement items are discussed quarterly with the managers responsible, thus monitoring the progress of the improvements. On this quality improvement list, findings from external quality audits are also gathered.

"It was first called the quality issue list, but as we thought that focusing on improvement opportunities would be more positive, we changed the name to the quality improvement list, in order to stimulate management to start using it."

This is one of the main issues that EDS is still working on, as with little resources and much effort needed to keep management attention at a high level, it proves quite hard to monitor constantly all improvement issues. The external auditor has therefore asked EDS to improve the resolution time of audit issues. The quarterly meetings are now being introduced, as well as a new traffic light report indicating which improvement issues are taking too long to be resolved (see Figure 1.3).

"The EDS enterprise as a whole is currently paying growing attention to this issue, so management commitment is now increasing."

Date:

Manager	Total Issues	Open			Closed		Completed
		Total open	On Time	Red	Green	Verified	
Manager 1	50	15	5	10	0	35	0
Manager 2	1	0	0	0	0	1	2
Manager 3	5	1	0	1	0	4	2
Manager 4	6	5	2	3	1	0	1
Manager 5	3	0	0	0	0	3	2
Manager 6	10	3	0	3	0	7	0
Manager 7	15	2	0	2	3	10	1
Manager 8	7	0	0	0	0	7	2
Manager 9	0	0	0	0	0	0	1
Manager 10	5	4	3	1	0	1	0
Manager 11	9	2	0	2	0	7	1
Manager 12	2	2	0	2	0	0	0
Manager 13	4	4	0	4	0	0	0
Manager 14	0	0	0	0	0	0	1
Manager 15	0	0	0	0	0	0	11
Manager 16	0	0	0	0	0	0	40
Manager 17	0	0	0	0	0	0	0
Total	117	38	10	28	4	75	107

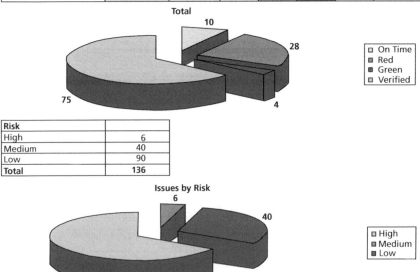

Risk	
High	6
Medium	40
Low	90
Total	136

Figure 1.3   Traffic light report indicating which improvement issues are taking too long to be resolved

1.9   External certification audit

Based upon the ISO 9001:2000 and the BS 15000 standard, the certification body conducted a five day audit of the management system, in February and April 2005. Due to some problems with scope definition, the BS 15000 certificate was not acquired in February 2005, with the ISO 9001 certificate, but in June 2005. This was turned into an ISO 20000 certificate in March 2006.

1.9.1   Gaps found

The external audit resulted into zero major and minor non conformances and almost twenty opportunities for improvement; they included:
- provide examples of how people are being informed
- review process KPIs for productivity tracking, quality (deviations in percentages) and trends
- think more about process improvements
- consolidate and communicate lessons learned
- process improvement regarding project management process (small items which can be done on country/region level)
- overall improvement plan: there are a lot of measurements, but the improvement plans are not always being embodied in the process
- create traffic light report for the IT service continuity process

1.9.2   Improvement actions started on these gaps

All findings are passed through to the owner and the owner is asked to make up an improvement plan. This is kept short, usually to a single page. It is checked to see whether the plan is actually followed and whether the planned improvements are being implemented.

Table 1.4 provides the template which EDS uses to make an improvement plan.

KEMA certification/surveillance audit issue Action Plan #	
Organization Name: ITO North	**Action Plan Date:** dd-mm-yyyy
Action Plan Type: KEMA certification/ surveillance audit issue	**Status Report Date(s):** dd-mm-yyyy
Action Owner(s): Name of owner	**Target Completion Date:** dd-mm-yyyy
Business Goals / Objectives:	Describe the action required and its status as stated by the audit report (major/minor non conformance, opportunity for improvement).
Action Details:	**Issue:** For example, an issue KEMA reported. **Root Cause:** Describe Root Cause **Action(s):** Actions needed
Target Result:	**Deliverables:** Describe deliverable **Measurement:** Describe how the deliverable can be measured, in order to be able to assess the issue and close it.

Action taken:	Proof per deliverable:
	Proof of the action taken (for example copy of e-mail sent or link to action list with countersigns of responsible people for actions actually being taken)

Table 1.4   Improvement plan template

These issues and improvement plans are incorporated into the quality improvement list mentioned in Section 1.8 (Internal audit), to ensure that they are being monitored and resolved within a reasonable period of time.

1.9.3   Converting the result into profit

As it was becoming more and more self-evident that EDS was maintaining a high quality level, the result was not formally celebrated.

In correspondence regarding RfPs, however, EDS mentions its ISO 20000 certificate, particularly when the companies that issue the tender request this in their RfP. The ISO 20000 certificate helped EDS to win tenders from two big international clients: Kraft Foods and the UK Ministry of Defence.

1.10   Preserving the certificate

Regarding awareness, metrics and reviews, agreements with line- and process management and the meeting structure on certification issues, the existing structure of the two dashboards and the weekly meetings to discuss shortcomings and their improvement plans have been maintained.

In order to maintain the certificates, the company added a dashboard to track the improvement actions that followed from the audits, in order to manage and control them better (see Section 1.8).

1.10.1   Interim audits

As the company has both the ISO 9001 and the ISO 20000 certificate, the third party auditing organization executes one surveillance audit for both standards every six months.

For each interim audit, EDS drafts a proposal on what subjects could be audited. An interim audit takes about two days, and a fixed part to be audited each time is the Quality Management System, results of internal audits, management and its organization. Besides this, there six other subjects can be audited, whether they are particular processes or organizational groups.

"Most important consideration is that all thirteen processes should at least be audited once in every three years. When this requirement has been met, we combine aspects of which we know are going well with subjects of which we think it would be good if an external person made a remark on the particular situation. If an external auditor mentions such a weak point, this helps to draw management attention and eventually provokes an improvement plan and improvement actions. Also, we try to audit different locations each time."

"When we've selected about eight audit subjects, we discuss these in teleconferences with the people involved, and see if they agree on our proposals, and if the Management Team has suggestions of their own."

This list is submitted to the auditor, and if he has suggestions, they are taken over in the audit plan. When the program of the interim audit has been agreed upon with the auditor, the people responsible for the processes being audited put together a presentation on the functioning of their process, based on the Plan-Do-Check-Act cycle. They describe their initial goal, what actions they have taken to achieve this goal, how they measure whether they have achieved it, and what actions still need to be taken to improve their future performance. During this presentation, the auditor will ask questions as they occur to him, to find out about the actual quality of the process. The manager responsible for the process being audited must also attend this meeting.

The auditors check whether people control their processes, rather than checking extensive procedures. Evidence required includes tools, databases, checklists, reports and improvement plans.

Also, major and minor conformities from previous audits are re-assessed, consulting the people owning these issues and their evidence.

1.10.2 Prepare for re-certification
Re-certification audits take five days and take place every three years. All processes are audited in such an assessment.

Although the company is quite experienced in being audited, it still is difficult to determine the extent to which they need to prove they have sufficient process control. With help of the auditor, EDS is investigating whether the level of detail can be determined as a constant factor. This would enable them to deliver just the right amount of evidence, in the right form. "The quality managers, being educated as registered IT Auditors themselves, help enormously in communicating with KEMA and understanding their needs for evidence and information."

The next assessment will be held in February 2008. Over the last two years EDS-ITO in the Netherlands has been incorporated into the HUB-organization for the region of North and Central Europe, comprising Scandinavia, Benelux, Austria, Switzerland, and other Eastern and Middle European countries. As a result of this, EDS Netherlands is currently preparing to extend the certificate's scope from the Netherlands, out to all of this area.

1.11 Evaluation of the business case
As described in Section 1.2.2, benefits and costs of the certification were not qualified, as quality certification is 'business as usual' within EDS. As mentioned in Section 1.9.3, however, one tangible benefit is that, due to the ISO 20000 certificate, EDS managed to win tenders from two big international clients, both of which required bidding organizations to have been ISO 20000 certified: Kraft Foods and the UK Ministry of Defence.

1.12 Project evaluation

"In the end, I think we've been rather too modest, instead of thinking too much that we'd already achieved the certification." Jan Boogers says. It turned out that EDS was indeed well on track for BS 15000 certification, and with heavy management commitment they managed to gain this certification successfully.

1.12.1 Company special message

Jan Boogers and Johan van Middelkoop believe their simple and pragmatic approach has eventually led them to successfully acquiring the ISO 20000 certificate: "We do not have a large quality staff, nor voluminous books or ever-lasting courses, but support our employees in embodying quality in their daily job. Within EDS, everybody is responsible for quality, and it's the quality manager's task to win the employees' minds and hearts and enhance quality awareness."

Absolutely essential for this success is strong and ongoing management commitment, which is sufficiently present within EDS. This case study presented examples of this, such as the commitment of the head of the management team in the teleconferences, and the highest executive phoning the responsible managers if their client dashboard was showing a red light. In addition, president and CEO of EDS, Ron Rittenmeijer, recently stated at the Chinese Institute of Engineers USA-DFW annual convention on August 25 2007:

> *"Flawless execution is critical to a company's success. Not just execution - it's flawless execution. We, for example, as I'm sure many of our competitors do, ensure that we have global standards for all tools and processes. We pay very strict attention to quality. We are a quality-first-driven company. It is something that will become part of our fabric, if it hasn't already, and will be something that we believe is the most important thing we do. We have a program called Zero Outages. When it was introduced a couple years ago, most people thought I was insane, and I may well be, but having said that, zero outages is what our customers pay us for."*

Zero outage is one of the key current initiatives within service delivery of EDS' Hub's. In essence, it is aimed at prevention of serious incidents (Severity 1 or 2) of Key Production Environments (KPE's).

Thus, by continually making people aware of their quality responsibility, and constantly renewing management commitment at a high level, EDS has managed to gain and preserve its ISO 20000 certificate since 2005.

Case 2
Fujitsu FIP Corporation

CASE DETAILS	(anonymized company is allowed)
Company name	Fujitsu FIP Corporation
Country	Japan
Year and Month of certification	March 2. 2007
Certification agency	Japan Quality Assurance Organization
Author of the case history	Masumi Taira
Role of author	ITSM Manager
Company of author	Administration Department
Date of case logging	May 7, 2007

2.1   Organization type

Company name	Fujitsu FIP Corporation
Established	November 28, 1977
Line of business	Information services
Head office	Time 24 Building Aomi Koto-ku Tokyo Japan
Branches, branch offices	Hamamatsucho, Osaka, Sapporo, Sendai, Nagoya, Hiroshima, Fukuoka, Morioka, Otawara, Saitama, Tachikawa, Yokohama, Nagano, Wakayama, Matsue
Number of Employees (as of April 1, 2006)	2,563
Capital	¥2.0 billion (wholly owned subsidiary of Fujitsu Ltd., which is a leading provider of customer-focused information technology and communications solutions for the global marketplace)
Sales	¥86.5 billion (FY2005)
Closing date	March 31

Table 2.1   Outline information on Fujitsu FIP

2.1.1   Organizational size

Within the scope of IT Service Management (ITSM) activities, the outsourcing services division (data center division) and EDI services division are the most relevant areas. IT outsourcing customers can be found in over 500 companies, and EDI service clients number in the tens of thousands. Figure 2.1 shows the Fujitsu FIP organization chart.

Table 2.2 shows personnel numbers in departments involved in ITSM activities. Personnel totals include outsourcing staff. Outsourcing staff represent 58.7% of the overall total.

2.1.2   Main activities

As an information services company, our main activities are IT outsourcing services, web services and system integration services:

- **IT outsourcing services** - We provide a full range of services, from infrastructure and operations, including optimal system resources and various networks, to system planning, application development and advanced operations management. Furthermore, we provide support for customer information system operations, with centers in 13 locations around Japan featuring advanced security environments (ISMS-certified, etc.), 24-hour year-round operations, and services provided by dedicated system engineers.
- **Web services** - We provide advanced, cutting-edge technologies and highly reliable, optimized network solutions for the broadband era, including EC/EDI services that support B2B transactions, primarily for the distribution and manufacturing industries, and various ASP services that provide groupware and business process applications.
- **System integration services** - We combine cutting-edge, specialized technologies with ample business process expertise in a range of industries, including public works, medicine, welfare, financial services, manufacturing, distribution, environmental services, and civil engineering, and software with hardware, to provide customers with optimized solutions.

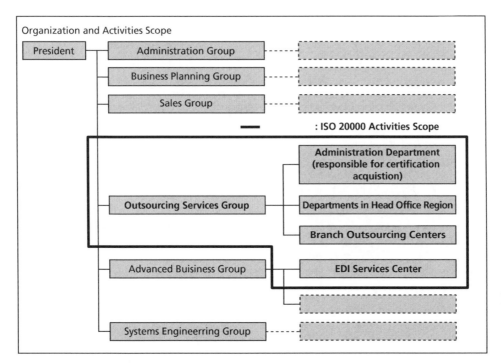

Figure 2.1   Fujitsu FIP organization chart

Business Office	Personnel
Tokyo Center	478
Business Operations Center	122
BPO Center	176
EDI Service Center	71
Yokohama Center	123
Shin-Yokohama Office	13
Time 24 Building	7
Osaka Center (Senri, Akashi)	210
Hokkaido Outsourcing Center	21
Tohoku Outsourcing Center	35
Nagano Outsourcing Center	8
Chubu Outsourcing Center	27
Chugoku/Shikoku Outsourcing Center	26
Kyushu Outsourcing Center	16
Customer Sites (multiple places)	340

Table 2.2   Personnel numbers in different offices

2.1.3   Relevance of IT Service Management

As indicated in Section 2.1.2, IT outsourcing services constitutes one of our three main services and is positioned as a core business.

By implementing ITSM we are striving to improve service quality further and to raise customer satisfaction through synergies with our quality control management system, information security management system, privacy management system and environmental management system. We want to utilize ITSM as a tool to help us to reach our business goals.

2.1.4   Customers

All of the organizational activities included within the scope of certification were IT services aimed at customers. The scope of activities covered planning, development, construction and operation of IT outsourcing services, and web services (EC/ASP services) provided to external customers (on the open market).

2.2   Drivers for certification

It is our duty, as an information services provider, to work to improve the quality of IT services and customer satisfaction.

We decided to utilize the IT Service Management system in addition to those of our other management systems that have already been certified (quality, security, environment, privacy). We anticipated that acquiring certification would provide an evaluation from an objective, independent perspective. At the same time, we sought to distinguish ourselves from providers who have not yet been certified.

2.2.1   Main initiator

The executive in charge of the outsourcing business, and the Management System Promotion Department in the Outsourcing Services Group (belonging to the Administration Department) were the first to propose the acquisition of ISO 20000 certification. This was included in the business plan for the fiscal year, 2006, as one of the measures for improving quality.

The decision to start this initiative was made at the business plan review meeting in April 2006. Actualization and promotion was managed by the Administration Department, as a part of its everyday activities.

2.2.2   Business case

Quantitative estimates were not made (the initiative was conducted within the annual budget; there is an existing system for managing budgets for each customer service).

It was decided that the scope of certification activities would be IT outsourcing services and EC/ASP services provided to customers; consequently, the benefits of certification would be to obtain an objective evaluation of IT services and to enhance PDCA activities at project sites (reviewing and improving services from an ITSM perspective, while they are being provided). It was concluded that improvements to our current management systems would be commensurate with the overall cost of the project.

2.2.2.1 Benefits

Having considered the general benefits of the project, we set the same quantified targets that existed for the Quality Management System (QMS) and the Information Security Management System (ISMS). Our targets were to cut the incidence of problems by 50% (when compared to the previous year), and to eliminate all security incidents or major problems. This 'cost cut by trouble reduction' was estimated to be around ¥50 million.

Certification would enable us to promote the quality of our IT services (raising the level of trust placed in the company) and exchange information with the promotion department in our parent company, which had already acquired certification for the same services.

Certification would help clarify IT services and service reports for customers (service transparency), thereby raising levels of trust and satisfaction in the company's services.

Across all IT services, certification would help to deepen recognition of the importance of operations, and raise satisfaction with the managers involved, by making operations work transparent and promoting continual improvement.

Management benefits were anticipated:
- Certification would allow IT services to be addressed from the perspective of business planning, business risk and finances.
- We had already implemented a QMS, but certification would enable us to clarify several processes related to operations which were not specified in the QMS (for example, change management, configuration management, release management, financial management for IT services, and IT service risk assessment).
- Certification would allow us to examine services, quality, malfunctions and 'trouble' from a broader perspective than from just the QMS (such as business strategy, recognition of business risk and management in terms of accounting).

Business benefits were also anticipated:
- Certification would allow us to promote the fact that we have a functioning IT Service Management system for development, operations and maintenance services, with a top level of quality and reliability.
- Certification would allow us to show a case study to customers in promoting sales of certification acquisition services as an offered service.
- Certification would enable us to engage in sales talks (enter bids) on projects requiring ITSM certification.

2.2.2.2 Costs

In the case of Fujitsu, certification was acquired after other management systems had been implemented and become operational; thus internal costs and external costs have been separated out to show how they were applied:

With regard to *acquisition costs*, we can distinguish the following:
- **Internal costs**:
  - *research on conformity among management systems (equivalent to assessment)*: one man-month

- – *ITSM documentation and distribution*: three man-months (including changes to other management system documents)
- – *training and propagation*: twice for each department; two to three hours per session
- – *development of system operation onsite*: differs with each department
- – *communications*: co-ordination with the certification agency conducted as necessary through meetings, reviews and emails
- – *internal auditing*:
  - ♦ auditing plan, auditing preparation, auditing report, correction flow: three man-months (dedicated staff)
  - ♦ confirmation of auditing basis and interviews: four hours
- • **External costs**:
  - – *auditing fees*: approximately ¥3.5 million (differs within the scope)

Running costs recognized were:
- • **registration fee/regulation audit fee** - ¥2.5 million
- • **staff in charge of promotion (personnel costs for dedicated staff)** - equivalent to one dedicated staff member/month, assuming the dedicated staff member is in charge of co-ordination with outside organizations, auditing planning and audit reports
- • **internal auditing** - four hours + travel costs
- • **training** - training materials, preparation time and training hours
- • **communications (meetings)** - two hours X number of times X attendees + travel costs

2.3   Quality management at the start of the project

In conjunction with quality improvement initiatives conducted throughout the Fujitsu Group, as the data center division, we acquired ISO 9001 certification for outsourcing services in the Tokyo area in October 1999 (not for any specific customer), and then acquired the 2000 version certification at all nationwide data centers in October 2002.

Certification of data center services started with outsourcing services in October 1999 and was expanded to all data center service processes by 2005, covering everything from contractual agreements, design, development and construction, to operations and maintenance services.

In December 2001, coinciding with the beginning of the ISMS system (Japan's conformity assessment scheme for information security management systems based on an ISMS certification standard, based in turn on the British BS 7799), and with reference to data center security, we acquired certification for outsourcing services at the Tokyo Center and at the Business Operations Center, expanding certification to all centers in 2003. The scope of application was also expanded to cover all data center services (outsourcing services in the form of hosting services, housing services, network connectivity services, operations management services, business process operations services, software design and development, and maintenance services).

We were involved in the early stages of the 'ISO-ization' of ISMS, and by December 12, 2006 had switched over to ISO 27001 certification for information security management systems (ISMS) at all ten centers nationwide (the largest scope of certification in Japan), and also acquired information security management certification in conformance with the international standard. Switchover activities were conducted in parallel with the activities to acquire ISO 20000 certification.

2.3.1   IT Service Management methods established

The data center division (including EC/ASP services) had been involved in the standardization of development and operations for some time. When we implemented the QMS, we focused on process standardization and the customer's perspective, and we succeeded in advancing standardization. Since 2002 we have standardized processes provided in IT services and in specific, individual work processes on an ITIL basis to provide transparency.

As far as the methodology for IT Service Management is concerned, we have been a member of itSMF-Japan since its establishment in 2002, and have actively collected information and researched case studies overseas. As an initiative of the overall Fujitsu Group, we have learned autonomously and have incorporated the best practices of other systems.

We do not simply implement individual processes; we look at existing processes from an ITIL perspective, and incorporate processes where there are deficiencies.

We had implemented ITIL for outsourcing services (including EC/ASP services) at data centers where QMS and ISMS had already been established. For this reason, we proceeded by linking ITSM processes to QMS/ISMS processes, implemented processes in areas of deficiency and redefined processes that needed conceptual clarification.

For example, we had a deficiency in the 'budgeting and accounting for IT services' process which is not recognized by ITIL, but which is acknowledged by ISO 20000. We conceptually redefined the processes for incident management, configuration management, change management, release management and service reporting. Consequently, no new tools needed to be implemented.

2.4   Parties involved

There was co-ordination with top management at the parent company, which already had certification. The executive in charge of the scope of certification activities (the managing director of the data center division) was positioned as the manager, and dedicated staff were appointed to be in charge of management system promotion at the Administration Department of the data center division (Administration Department). The QMS was also handled within the same organizational structure; the QMS manager was the same person.

2.4.1   Management staff

We addressed the certification within the existing organization, with certification on the agenda of the QMS/ISMS promotion meeting held in September 2006. The aim of this meeting was to promote management system goals, make ongoing improvements and hold discussions. It was attended by supervisors and staff, including upper level management. The start of activities for acquiring ISO 20000 certification was formally approved at this meeting.

2.4.2   Employees
Employees were informed of the results of the committee's deliberations (meeting minutes), utilizing communication systems such email and the web, and by holding meetings with management review participants in September 2006.

2.4.3   Customers
There were no special announcements to customers regarding the start of the initiative. Prior to the initiative, we had communicated the importance of service level agreements and service reports by working to set numerical targets in the agreements. On our website, we announced that we were currently working to earn ISO 20000 certification in the second half of the fiscal year, 2006.

2.4.4   Subcontractors
Companies primarily involved in work inside our offices participated in the presentations and notifications cited in 1.4.2. No special briefings were conducted for any other companies. Contractual clauses at the time were adequate to cover the ongoing work.

2.4.5   Third parties
We did not conduct any special measures for these types of organizations. In August 2006 we exchanged information with the parent company department responsible for providing IT services (the department that conducted activities ahead of us and acquired certification in August 2006).

2.5   Initial assessment
We did not use external consultants for the assessment work. Since we had already implemented a QMS/ISMS, the responsibility of the Administration Department was limited to linking the systems to ISO 20000 (confirming conformity)which; this was conducted instead of assessment. Comparisons with QMS/ISMS activities themselves were positioned as the assessment.

Accordingly, the scope was the same as the QMS' scope, the project was handled by the QMS/ISMS promotion Department (Administration Department) with its four current staff members, internal auditing was conducted in concert with QMS auditing, management reviews were conducted simultaneously with QMS/ISMS reviews and with gaps in processes between QMS/ISMS activities actually being conducted. ITSM requirements also were assessed by identifying processes defined by the QMS and by any excess or deficiencies in the ITSM processes.

Specifically, a checklist was created for each of the ISO 20000 requirements to ensure the existence of processes (whether the processes are defined in the QMS/ISMS) and of documents or records describing the activities. Those that existed were entered into the checklist. In this way we confirmed processes on a requirement-by-requirement basis.

We identified processes which were not defined in the QMS/ISMS, discrepancies in the scope of terminology, use of different terminology and other differences; these were incorporated into ITSM documentation (we created a new ITSM manual in order to make it the standard for ITSM activities).

A summary of these gaps were reported, together with the certification acquisition schedule, at the QMS/ISMS promotion meeting in September, and we obtained the agreement of everyone involved in the processes.

We were already conducting budget management and risk assessments on services as part of the company's organizational management, so we proceeded by including these in the ISO management system. Specifically, we included the management of documents and records for these activities in the ITSM manual.

They were also included in onsite training and training materials after the ITSM manual was issued.

During onsite training, we emphasized that:
- Risk assessment is conducted with respect to information assets under the ISMS, so the scope of risk assessment differs between ITSM and ISMS; ITSM takes up a broader scope of risk, assessments are not limited to information assets, and business risk is subject to assessment.
- Release management is not limited to hardware, software and networks.
- Configuration management is not limited to device architecture, network architecture and software architecture.
- The external audit also confirmed that these explanations were effective.

We added the following processes:
- IT service budgeting and accounting
- risk assessment on services

We clarified the release management process, and reformulated terms such as:
- **Incident** - any event which is not part of the standard operation of a service and which causes or may cause an interruption to, or a reduction in, the quality of that service; it also includes the change in the product environment, such as work system change or work procedure change, including documents related to the change
- **Release** - a phase change and production environment change from the planning or testing phase according to the QMS
  (Note: This is only applicable to the services that are offered by the outsourcing service HQ.)
- **Service desk** - in the outsourcing service headquarters, it points at an organization or a function having a customer facing function as regards the relevant service

2.6   Decision to go for certification

In relation to data center services, we had decided from the beginning to align the scope of certification with the QMS.

The formal decision by the Outsourcing Services Group was made at the QMS/ISMS promotion meeting held in September.

The decision by Fujitsu FIP was made when the Management Committee (deliberative body for management issue made up of the president, managing officers and corporate auditors) took up the decision of the Outsourcing Services Group, and granted approval for concluding an auditing agreement, acquiring certification upon finalizing the auditing schedule and fee with the certification agency, and the auditing fee itself (November 2006).

2.6.1 Scope

The scope of ITSM was the same as the QMS which was already in operation at the Outsourcing Services Group. Table 2.3 shows which services are included in the scope (indicated by o). A separate and different QMS certification has been acquired by the systems division for the data center division for web service development and system integration service development.

Business Classification (Development and Operations)	Service Subject to ITSM
IT outsourcing services: development	o
IT outsourcing services: operations	o
Web services: development	-
Web services: operations	o
System integration services: development	-

Table 2.3   Services included in the scope (o = included)

The scope of the QMS's registration included:
- **outsourcing services**:
  - hosting and housing services
  - network connection services
  - operations management services
  - business process operation services
  - software design, development and maintenance
  - operations management for electronic commerce and application service provider (ASP) services
- **ITSM's registration** - the Service Management System supporting the outsourced services managed from the Kanagawa office, including Hosting and Housing Services, Network Services, Business Process Operation Services, Operation Management Services, Electronic Commerce Service, Application Services and Provision Services

As with the QMS and ISMS, ITSM activities were conducted at the head office and branch office departments responsible for services related to the outsourcing services division (See Section 2.1.1).

However, at the time of the audit, the service menu offered differed, depending on the business office, so each office conducted specific activities for the particular services that they were providing.

Standards and procedures for service provisions had been standardized in the QMS documentation, so each department documented only those procedures unique to their department.

2.6.2   Objective

The target for the fiscal year, 2006 was to acquire certification, but as a business target, we sought to differentiate ourselves from other companies. Organizationally, we sought to utilize certification as a tool for developing internal controls for IT governance and IT departments, and as a tool for improving quality, reliability and customer satisfaction for our IT services.

2.6.3   Organization

The four-member group, in charge of promoting management systems in the Administration Department within the Outsourcing Services Group, handled the project. All members of the group are employees of the company, and they include one manager. We did not utilize outside resources such as consultants.

The internal personnel acquired knowledge about ITSM by attending training sessions on ISO 20000 conducted by training organizations, and by reading publications. We attended conferences held by itSMF-Japan and utilized information obtained from participating as a member in subcommittee meetings (the research committee, participated in voluntarily by itSMF-Japan members).

For internal auditing, the lead auditor for QMS (who was not a member of the four-person promotion group) also served as the lead auditor for ITSM, and efforts were made to enable auditing expertise to be utilized.

2.6.4   Funding

Examination fees and internal auditing-related costs were incorporated into the budget for the fiscal year, 2006, when the budget was created. There were no new tools that needed to be procured in connection with implementing ITSM, so no budget was allocated for facilities.

The promotion organization itself handled certification with its existing organizational structure, so no staff were added, other than to replenish shortages called for in personnel plans.

2.6.5   Action and time plan

Table 2.4 shows the schedule from the moment the decision to acquire certification was made until certification was achieved. The information was taken from promotion meeting documents.

2.6.6   Communication plan

The communication plan followed a policy of utilizing the QMS and ISMS communication system that had already been established.

The system includes regular meetings (management review, promotion committee, etc.), group training and briefings, an intranet portal site and email, to publicize and communicate management systems.

The principal means of communication used at each step of ITSM promotion were as follows:
- **planning (project launch)** - reports and deliberations by the promotion committee
- **operation (conducting ITSM processes)** - conducted group training and briefings at each business office

		2006			2007		
	Sep	Oct	Nov	Dec	Jan	Feb	Mar
Until September: **promotion group preparation period**							
Request quotation from certification agency; contractual procedures for examination	Δ						
Create ITSM manual (positioned as basic manual)	⟶						
Revise QMS procedures (to reflect ISO 20000 requirements)	⟶						
October: **start activities at each department**							
Issue ITSM documents and revised QMS documents		Δ					
Briefings on certification acquisition, visits		⟶					
December: **internal auditing**							
Internal auditing conducted at the same time as internal H2 QMS auditing				⟶			
December: **Preliminary survey**				Δ			
Preliminary confirmation of system development and ITSM documents by certification agency							
January: **Management review/external audit (1st)**							
Mid to late January: Conduct management review (as ITSM)					Δ		
Mid to late January: External audit (first stage; mainly documents)					Δ		
February: **External audit (2nd)**							
External audit (second stage; onsite examination)						Δ	
Submission of correction plan for problems indicated and correction activities						⟶	
March: **Acquisition of certification**							Δ

Table 2.4   Schedule until certification

- **inspection (internal auditing)** - conducted on an advisory basis at the same time as QMS audits with the auditors in charge of promotion
- **improvement (corrections, prevention, management review)** - communication of preventive measures utilized the portal site; operating status was reported in the management review
- **auditing via the certification agency** - findings reported at the promotion meeting; audit minutes posted on portal site
- **certification acquisition** - publicized on the company-wide intranet bulletin board

2.7   Preparation for certification

In accordance with the initial plan, we proceeded through audit application, audit contracting and the preliminary audit in December. When the certification agency had confirmed the certification scope, audit schedule, and status of ITSM construction, the actual audit followed, with a document audit in January and the onsite audit in February, with the promotion group leading the way.

Progress made was conveyed to each department through the QMS and ISMS management review in October, the QMS and ISMS promotion meeting in December, and emails and portal site postings by the promotion group.

Visits to departments to prepare for the onsite audit incorporated the findings of the first stage of the audit, so they primarily took place in mid-January and were conducted around two months later than initially planned.

2.7.1   Selection of the certification agency
We chose the agency that had already certified the QMS and ISMS for the data center division, the Japan Quality Assurance Organization (JQA).

This decision was based on our assessment of examination and examiner quality, and because, starting in the fiscal year, 2007, we are planning to integrate the QMS and ISMS certification, which we already have, with ITSM, into a single management system, in order to consolidate and improve the efficiency of maintenance, improvement and auditing.

We also hoped that by using the same certification agency it would facilitate greater communication with that organization.

2.7.2   Determine scope with certification agency
The certification scope was made the same as for the QMS and ISMS, which we were already involved in, and no particular issues needed to be adjusted with the certification agency.

One of the organizations involved, the EDI Service Center, was outside of the scope of ISMS certification at the beginning of ITSM activities, so we explained to the certification agency that we had started ISMS activities for ITSM security requirements from October 2006, and that we would expand the scope at the next regular ISMS audit (scheduled for September 2007).

The departments subject to auditing in the second stage were adjusted.

Onsite services were subject to the accreditation process (in the case that services were being provided at the customer site, the audit would be limited to sites where prior approval from the customer had been obtained).

January and February are busy months for our industry, so some departments did not have sufficent time to accommodate an audit (when data centers were in the midst of moving and when switching over to the live environment for large-scale systems), and some departments had planned events (opening ceremony for a new business office) and wished to put off the examination until after the event had taken place.

The schedule was co-ordinated with the certification agency in advance, in the light of these considerations.

2.7.3   Collecting data on the management system

Data collection was divided into data to be collected by the promotion group and onsite records indicating records of activities. This data was collected via email, intranet bulletin boards and internal mail.

The department handling promotion managed the following items as meeting documentation:
1. overviews of progress versus targets within each department
2. findings of analyses of incident occurrence, causes, countermeasures and rectification status
3. status of preventive measures within each department (cumulative results of the individual activities of each department summarized by the promotion group)
4. internal auditing status, external auditing status, response to issues indicated (summarized by the promotion group)
5. other topics such as new technology and service trends, issues requiring information to be communicated and event info

The following items were managed via a common information site:
1. risk assessment tables for the information assets of each department
2. business continuity plans for each department
3. QMS targets and progress reports (quarterly) for each department
4. ISMS targets and progress reports (quarterly) for each department
5. status of incident occurrence and corrective/preventive activities for each service and at each site
6. documents and minutes from each meeting

Each department registered this data and reported the status of activities to the committee.

For data on the customers of each service, documents and records were organized by customer managers. They managed the service implementation status for each customer in an integrated manner. The following are the activities of departments, and summarize those documents and records:
1. progress against QMS/ISMS targets and measures taken if not yet achieved
2. status of revision and rectification for issues indicated in internal auditing or external audits
3. initiatives related to customer satisfaction
4. implementation of disaster and safety measures
5. initiatives for customer processes with frequent incidence of 'trouble'

2.7.4   Establish service improvement plan

We proceeded in accordance with the schedule indicated in Section 2.6.5. There were no issues that required the creation of an improvement plan.

Improvement activities were limited to describing insufficiencies in existing management activities in the ITSM manual, and explaining and seeking understanding regarding discrepancies in terminology and process meanings, by visiting each department and holding training sessions and presentations.

For these visits, we drew up a list of potential questions and answers during the onsite audit, and sought understanding regarding the work (functions) that each individual and department was responsible for and the connection with ITSM requirements (we distributed materials and made presentations from January onwards).

Examples of potential questions:
- **ITSM policy/objectives**:
    - What is the policy of the Chief Executive Officer (CEO)?
    - What do you think about the policy from an ITSM viewpoint?
    - What is the target of your section/project?
    - What is being achieved?
    - Is there any measure which is considered when your target is not achieved?
- **Recognition of a business risk**:
    - What is the role of your section?
    - What is the risk that your section, a project, or a service must control?
    - What kind of risk do you manage?
    - What kind of risks do you find?
      (Note that the ISMS's risk management plan is mainly for the information assets. This is a question for recognizing business risks rather than security risks.)
    - How is the risk management plan formed?
    - How do you respond to a critical risk that is found in the plan?
- **Management of the SLA**:
    - How do you propose agreements for the SLA as a project/section leader?
    - Who are the customers?
    - How do you measure/report on the SLA agreements?
    - Is the SLA being adjusted according to 'change management'?

The following two points were highlighted as future issues:
- The need onsite for consolidation of management systems was further clarified. When visiting the departments to give presentations, there were specific requests from administrative staff for materials that explained the relationship and discrepancies with the QMS, in order to explain them in turn to department members.
- Construction of a system for configuration management, including the implementation of tools, was necessary, for promptly delivering the necessary information to the people and places that needed it. We provide services by dividing organizations by function, so they can provide their respective functions to one customer. Therefore, the people involved are spread across multiple departments and sites. We therefore face the issue of promptly conveying changes to the system configuration to the necessary people.

The *owner* of the service improvement plan was the ITSM manager. He was responsible for promoting ITSM certification. He created documents, passed them out to the departments, created a schedule for onsite visits, and assigned promotion group members to give presentations to the individual departments.

Confirmation that presentations had been conducted within departments according to plan was given, along with the names of attendees. This was handled as a part of everyday work (part of the annual work plans for the departments), without the need for a business case.

2.8   Internal audit

The internal audit was included in the regular auditing (twice yearly) conducted with the QMS.

The 2006 internal auditing plan created and approved by management in May was revised in November (conformance with ISO 20000 requirements was added to the scope of auditing). After the revised plan was re-approved by management, issues pertaining to ISO 20000 were checked in the audit for the second half of the fiscal year, 2006:

- Onsite auditing was conducted from the beginning of December 2006 to the middle of January 2007.
- Fourteen departments were checked. We were careful to check one or more departments for each service.
- Auditors with substantial ITSM knowledge were selected among qualified QMS internal auditors.
- For the audits, discrepancies in judgment among the auditors were minimized by creating a checklist of the issues to be checked. Teams of two auditors conducted the audits.
- Audit findings were reported at the management review held in January 2007.

Because this was the first internal audit, most of the internal auditors were also involved in certification promotion, and ISO 20000 requirements were explained during the course of the audit.

Regarding the examination of the same work from an ITSM perspective (rather than a QMS perspective), the understanding of the departments was a step away from where it needed to be; for example, documents and record management objects are in fact part of configuration information, and final inspections and delivery are in fact part of release management.

Categories of issues indicated by the internal audit:

- **organizations audited**: 14
- **case of nonconformance**:
  - *major deficiencies* - 0
  - *minor deficiencies* - 1: inappropriate access authorization for tools provided internally
- **Observations** - 7

There were no new measures initiated in response to the audit findings. We steadily carried out awareness-raising activities, so that those directly involved onsite would be able to understand and compare the ITSM requirements with their own everyday work, and be able to explain them to a third party.

2.9   External audit

The external audit was conducted in February 2007 and was divided into a first stage and a second stage (Table 2.5). The manager in charge and the internal audit counted as a single department, and the interview with top management counted as a single department.

We received confirmation from the auditing body that the certification had been registered as of

Audit stage	Audit period	Auditing man-hours	Auditors	Departments audited	Issues indicated
1st (documents)	1/23-24	3 man-days	2	7	0
2nd (onsite)	2/19-23	13 man-days	3	25	0

Table 2.5   External audit stages

March 2 and a certificate attesting to the fact of registration.

2.9.1   Gaps found

Two strong points were indicated in the 2nd stage audit. No nonconformances (issues indicated for improvement) were found in the 1st or 2nd stages. However, some opportunities for improvement were identified:

* **1st stage** - 1: regarding internal auditor knowledge of ITSM
* **2nd stage** - 9:
    - 4 pertaining to incident management and problem management
    - 3 pertaining to configuration management
    - 1 pertaining to service reports
    - 1 pertaining to SLA

We were evaluated as having made no major oversights. However, it was suggested that we consider a guide to facilitate the consistency of handling by staff at the work level, in terms of what should be regarded as an incentive; how much the results of evaluations and analysis of recognized events should be managed as configuration information; management methods for internal documents; and customer reports.

2.9.2   Improvement actions started on these gaps

No issues requiring improvement were indicated, so special improvement actions have not been initiated.

In the form of normal management system maintenance and continual improvement activities, we are conducting reviews and revision of work at departments where improvement opportunities were indicated, and providing instructions to the departments through promotion meetings (horizontal development) on how to respond to the same event.

2.9.3   Converting the result into profit

As of April 2007, we have publicized the certification within the company, informed the parent company, and announced it to the media. We have not conducted any analyses regarding profit.

When the certificate was won, it was communicated by a variety of means:
* **Internal communication**:
    - *data center division* - e-mail
    - *company-wide* - intranet bulletin board

- **External communication**:
  - *parent company* - e-mail
  - *general* - press release (April 2)
- **Marketing actions**:
  - posted on the company's public website
  - requesting inclusion in data center service pamphlet/catalog
  - certification mentioned in service catalogs
  - display copies of registration certificates at the entrance to relevant offices
  - added ISO 20000 certification to presentation during data center tours
  - indicated certification on the business cards of relevant employees
  - posted on the certifying body's website (Japan Quality Assurance Organization, www.jqa.jp/cgi-bin/06manage/14_touroku/result_j.cgi) and the itSMF-UK website (www.isoiec20000certification.com/lookupdetail.asp?LookupID=171)

We planned trouble reduction as a measure and as a result the cash on benefits are worth approximately 20 million ¥. On the other hand, however, we did not take qualitative analysis effect, such as the satisfaction of employee and stakeholders, into account.

At the first nationwide meeting (sales meeting) of the fiscal year held on April 23, 2007, the group general manager was honored and an award certificate and cash award was allocated. The cash award was distributed to departments within the scope of the certification activities. In the category for quality and compliance in the fiscal year, 2006, the fact that we had petitioned to acquire ISO 20000 certification in conjunction with the switch to ISO 27001 was assessed highly by the company as a whole.

2.10 Preserving the certificate

As a data center business, improving the quality of IT services is of the utmost importance. Accordingly, certification has ongoing importance; we plan to utilize it as a tool for providing and improving services in line with the intent of the standard.

2.10.1 Awareness

The system will be operated utilizing the same management system mechanisms as the QMS and ISMS. However, in order to improve the efficiency of maintenance management onsite, we plan to consolidate these three certifications in the fiscal year, 2007. The promotional body for maintenance management will be the same as before: dedicated staff responsible for promotion will be assigned within the Administration Department.

2.10.2 Metrics and reviews

Ongoing measurements will be conducted by synchronizing them with other management system activities. Monitoring will be conducted by utilizing mechanisms that include internal audits of management systems, external audits, self-checks, confirmation of progress against targets (promotion meetings), and management reviews.

2.10.3 Agreements with line- and process management

We will pay close attention to the opportunities that were indicated for improvement, even in departments not subject to the indications.

2.10.4 Meeting structure on certification issues
The Administration Department handles certification issues as described in 2.10.1. The promotion meeting and management review act as regular opportunities at which these issues can be discussed.

2.10.5 Interim audits
Internal audits are planned for each fiscal year, so additional internal audits were not planned for the fiscal year, 2006.

2.10.6 Prepare for re-assessment
There are no plans for reassessment in the fiscal year, 2006. In activity after 2007, we plan to review internal audit items and ITSMS documents based on the review logs and points that are indicated.

2.11 Evaluation of the business case
We only finalized business costs. We have not ascertained other costs other than trouble-related costs (because a special budget was not established).

2.11.1 Actual benefits
Against our goal of reducing the incidence of 'trouble' by half (for services provided to customers), in the fiscal year, 2006, trouble fell by 17% on the previous year; this represents the equivalent of approximately ¥20 million in response costs.

2.11.2 Real costs
We have not conducted a detailed analysis, but the costs for implementing ITSM were within the estimated range (based on the fact that man-hours were not excessive and plans were not delayed with respect to customer services).

2.11.3 Ultimate appraisal of the business case
The fact that we acquired certification without any improvement indications reflected well on our daily activities, and managers and departmental personnel were satisfied with this.

However, while there were no formal problems or problems with the general framework, there is variance in development and management within individual customer services. Issues requiring ongoing improvement by managers and promotional staff did arise.

As for the formal appraisal of the project as a whole, the project was recognized as an activity to improve quality and the group general manager was honored.

2.12 Project evaluation
We completed acquisition of the certification in the second half of the fiscal year, 2006 as initially planned, so we grade the project as a success.

Among the critical success factors were:
- strong support from top management
- specialization of promotional staff (efficiency improved by appointing staff who were also in charge of other management systems)
- experience with and continuation of QMS, ISMS and other management systems
- support and co-operation of frontline departments in acquiring certification
- minimal ITSM documentation (only documented relation with other management systems and additions)

There were no major problems.

In terms of areas that were adjusted, we were requested to provide a presentation during onsite training, on the differences and relationship with QMS activities, that would be easy to understand for those immediately involved. Figures 2.2 and 2.3 show some of the presentation materials.

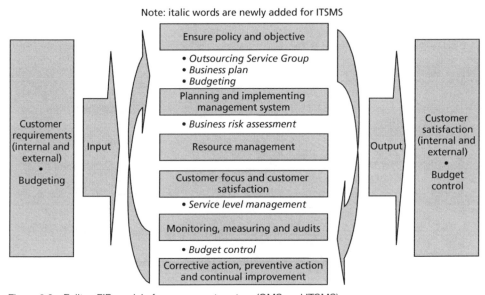

Figure 2.2   Fujitsu FIP model of management system (QMS and ITSMS)

Because all staff members involved (including onsite management and leaders) understood issues related to the maintenance and continual improvement of management systems, the basics of PDCA were firmly rooted (responding to requirements, conducting activities by setting goals, the need for auditing, correction and preventive activities).

Based on this project, there are several main concerns when implementing ISO 20000:
- When a management system is being implemented for this first time, it is necessary to first ensure that frontline personnel understand the structure of the system (processes and PDCA).

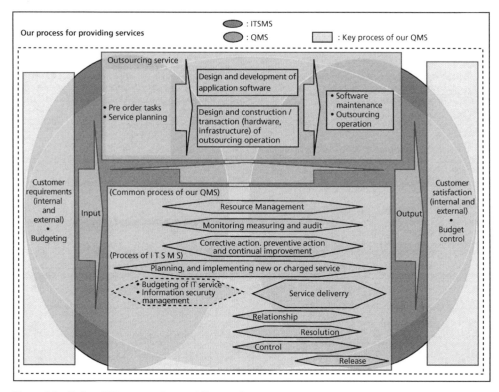

Figure 2.3   Fujitsu FIP process for providing services

- If procedures for IT services have not been standardized, it is likely to take some time to understand the actual operating situation for the services, and there may be some friction with frontline personnel.
- The extent of strong support from top management, including management resources, needs to be anticipated. Is a group being created to be in charge of promotion, are staff members going to be assigned on a dedicated basis?

2.12.1 Company special message

If a company is utilizing IT to conduct business, IT services are being managed in some fashion; so organizing their implementation in line with the requirements of ISO 20000 should make it possible to implement the IT services management system in order to fill in any gaps. If a management system is already in place (ISO 9001 in particular), this standard is fairly easy to tackle. We recommend utilizing it not only as a best practice for organizing IT services, but also to help raise their quality.

Case 3:
ING Service Centre Budapest (SCB)

CASE DETAILS	(anonymized company is allowed)
Company name	ING Service Centre Budapest (SCB)
Country	Hungary
Year and Month of certification	November 2004
Certification body	DNV UK and Ireland
Author of the case history	Jaap van Staalduine and Gábor Patay
Role of authors	CEO and CIO
Company of author	ING Service Centre Budapest
Date of case logging	12-02-2007

IMPORTANT NOTE: While producing this book, in September 2007, the ING Service Center Budapest activities were migrated to ING Bank Romania. ING Romania has no certificate yet.

3.1   Organization type

ING Service Centre Budapest (SCB) is a shared service centre of ING Group N.V. for servicing ING Banks in Central Europe.

3.1.1   Organizational size

Table 3.1 gives some basic information on ING SCB.

Number of offices	1 (located in Budapest, Hungary)
Service provision	Multinational: Hungary, Romania, Ukraine, Slovakia, Czech Republic
Personnel in concerned business line	30
Financial information	Cost center of ING Group N.V. with cost plus model
Number of customers	5 ING Banks in Central Europe

Table 3.1   Outline information on ING SCB

3.1.2   Main activities

SCB's main business is the application service provision of an integrated retail banking system for the ING Banks in Central Europe. ING uses the Profile-Anyware system, developed by Fidelity National Information Services (FNIS). Profile-Anyware is a bank account keeping system with the following main functionalities:
- customer information file maintenance
- deposit account keeping
- loan account keeping
- teller
- domestic payment system
- FX payment system
- reporting

Profile-Anyware is interfaced to several other systems such as:
- card management system
- SWIFT
- local clearing system
- IVR
- internet banking

3.1.3   Relevance of IT Service Management

IT Service Management is a core business of SCB, which ensures efficient, effective and controlled service provision on SLA guaranteed quality and low cost level.

The Profile-Anyware banking system operation/support and development is a business critical service for the customers (ING Banks) of ING SCB, as this is the LOB system for retail banking. Its 7*24*365 operation is crucial for servicing the clients of the bank.

3.1.4 Customers

SCB services only ING Group N.V. internal customers, but as a separated legal entity it behaves partially as a third party provider. The customers of SCB are:

- ING Bank Hungary
- ING Bank Ukraine
- ING Bank Slovakia
- ING Bank Czech
- ING Bank Romania

3.2 Drivers for certification

The main drivers to achieve certification were:

- the ability to process large volumes of transactions (around 3m transactions per month, but growing continuously; max 100 TPS) at high quality (99.95% system availability 7*24*365, max. 1 sec response time) and low cost level
- to ensure high availability of on-line real time transaction processing
- to create outperforming company reputation, to show reliability and professionalism to customers

3.2.1 Main initiator

The quality improvement project was initiated when the business plan was approved. Formal certification was initiated by the management of the company, in order to demonstrate the quality of ING SCB to customers.

3.2.2 Business case

A formal business case was not made, given the existence of a strong need for quality improvement and the relatively low cost of implementation.

3.3 Quality management at the start of the project

At the start of the project, the only regulated, managed and documented process was the change management process. This was managed by an in-house developed Lotus Notes application. This application also managed formal communication with customers and users, and solved resource allocation issues. Other ITIL processes were also partly functional, but were not regulated or documented.

ING SCB already had a certified ISO 9001:2000 Quality Management System in place. The certification was achieved in early 2003.

3.4 Parties involved

The CEO and CIO (also Quality Manager) initiated the official certification of BS 15000. Sponsor of the project was the CIO, who followed up the implementation on a daily basis.

3.4.1   Management staff

At project start-up, the CEO and the CIO informed senior management of the aims of the project, as detailed at Section 3.2.

3.4.2   Employees

Process owners were selected and then all other staff were informed. All staff received ITIL Foundation training.

Process owners were formally appointed and everyone was informed that annual appraisals would evaluate the process owner work. Since ING SCB is a small organization, process owners were existing staff members working on the project on a part-time basis.

3.4.3   Customers

Customers were initially informed in a face-to-face meeting. A regular monthly newsletter was subsequently initiated.

Customer communication focused on the following topics:

- What are ITIL and IT Service Management?
- Why is implementation necessary?
- Why is implementation good for both the customer and the service provider?
- What will be the changes for the customer?
- What will be the main improvements for the customer?
- Project progress reporting
- Service catalogue development
- SLA development
- Signing of new SLA

3.5   Initial assessment

Self assessment was provided by third party consultants using the standard BS 15000 self assessment questionnaire. The consultants clarified terms and requirements to staff to enable the questionnaire to be completed.

A third party program manager and one process designer was on site for six months to guide internal staff.

The main finding of the initial assessment was that almost all IT Service Management processes were operational to a certain level, with the exception of service level management. The existing processes were based on the experience of the organization; they were self developed and they were not using best practices or other methodologies. These processes were not formalized or documented. The only exception to this was the change management process, which was well developed.

The self assessment was repeated midway through the process and also prior to the external audit. This proved to be very useful to identify the gaps. It also made the progress of the project more visible.

The initial assessment resulted in a 25% compliance with the BS 15000 requirements; the next assessment resulted in 50% compliance and the final one in 85% compliance to the standard.

3.6 Decision to go for certification

The company management decided to aim for certification, with the main driver being to reinforce success and quality to customers. Customers never asked for certification, but acknowledged it as a proof of quality. The certificate was used very successfully for PR and marketing purposes.

Timing of the certification was influenced by the following factors:
* going live with all IT Service Management processes
* **month of operation**
* more than 80% compliance in the BS 15000 assessment

3.6.1 Scope

The scope of the certification was:

> *service support and operation of banking application and infrastructure for ING Bank N.V. subsidiaries*

This is the main business focus (line) of the company; the smaller and non strategic ones were not involved.

3.6.2 Objective

The objectives of the certification were to:
* become able to process large transaction volumes at high quality and at a low cost level
* ensure high availability of online real time transaction processing
* increase organizational knowledge

3.6.3 Organization

A formalized project organization was established, as part of the quality improvement program. The program manager and project manager/ITIL consultant was a third party consultant. The project sponsor was the CIO. The project members were the process owners (internal). For this role, leaders and key specialists of the related process area were selected from the existing staff.

Generic Project Lifecycle (GPL), ING's proprietary project management methodology, was used to manage the project. It is based on a simplified version of PRINCE2™ and is customized to internal ING rules and policies.

3.6.4 Funding and resource plan

The project was financed by the ING Central Europe Regional Office. There were three external senior ITIL consultants involved and 10 internal employees.

External ITIL consultants drove the implementation process by:
* creating standard ITIL process descriptions
* sharing experience of previous projects

Process owners customized the standard ITIL processes according to ING SCB operations, and rolled out the new processes.

3.6.5   Action and time plan

Table 3.2 shows the time and action plan.

Period (month number)	Action
1-2	review current processes, find gaps compared to ITIL recommendations
3	develop new, ITIL aligned processes for discussion
4	ITIL Foundation training for all staff
5-6	fine tuning of processes, implementation of new Service Management tool
7	implementation of new processes
9	final review before audit

Table 3.2   Action and time plan

3.6.6   Communication plan

During the project, regular internal staff communication took place, including weekly meetings and sharing of the progress reports.

Staff communication encompassed:
* project start-up
* progress
* expected changes in the co-operation with SCB
* roll-out
* experiences
* certification

3.7   Preparation for certification

3.7.1   Selection of the certification agency

At the initiation of the project three companies were accredited for BS 15000 certification, two multi-national agencies and a specialized agent. An RfP was sent to the two multi-nationals. The services offered were the same, so price differential was a key selection criteria. The successful company was the one that had previously certified ING SCB for ISO 9001:2000.

3.7.2   Determine scope with certification agency

The scope was clear and unchanged from the beginning of the project. According to the ISO 20000 standard it covers all aspects of a specified business line. Other SCB business lines were intentionally excluded.

3.7.3   Collecting data on the management system

Original assessment was based on the following:
* procedures
* records of QMS
* interviews with the relevant staff

3.7.4   Establish service improvement plan

The existing processes were compared at a very detailed level to those anticipated according to ITIL best practice. The processes were reviewed to see whether they were operating according to the process definitions and whether quality records were being kept.

New processes were developed, as gaps between old and new processes were identified. The action plan was developed and executed to eliminate gaps and to implement new processes.

The introduction was structured, without any quick wins being identified or adopted. This was mainly due to the relatively small size of the organization and to the fast implementation of the complete Service Management system.

The main achievements of the project were the:
* introduction of a single point of contact, with full tracking of the calls in a Service Management system
* set up of a CMDB
* introduction of service level management (as internal supplier; it was not previously in existence)
* introduction of a new SLA structure with service catalogue
* introduction of service level reporting
* introduction of integrated processes for incident-, problem- and change management
* replacement of Service Management tool by an integrated one, incorporating all service support processes

These improvements were realized during the implementation phase of the new processes, including the replacement of the tooling.

The SIP was owned by the service level manager. The IT Service Manager and process owners were involved in the management of the SIP.

GPL was used for project management and progress monitoring. GPL is Generic Project Lifecycle, and it is ING's proprietary project management methodology.

3.8   Internal audit

Final internal assessment was done using BS 15000 self assessment sheets. Questions were answered by process owners and checked by external consultants. In December 2006, a one day annual review audit verified successful compliance to ISO 20000.

We had intended to eliminated all previously determined gaps, but minor follow-up actions were required. Some 'last-minute' actions were needed to adjust some process definitions and staff practice.

3.9   External audit

SCB was originally certified against the BS 15000 standard in November 2004. In his final judgment, the auditor spoke of a:

> *"good grasp by all staff of how the IT Service Management system and ITIL processes apply to their role".*

Most minor issues were identified from the internal audit, but they were not considered to be of critical importance.

The formal result of the audit identified four minor non conformances:
- the integration with the Quality System needed to be progressed
- the internal audit procedure had to be followed more clearly
- service reviews had to be fully implemented, including consideration of complaint status
- use of CCA (Competence Centre Assistant) should be improved with regard to maintaining the correct status of priority, disposition to the correct team and action entries for key SLA points

Positive indications were:
- a careful and considered approach taken to implementing the IT Service Management system
- good commitment to a formal improvement process that was clearly well supported
- automation of IT Operations via the OPERUS tool allowing for careful control of the large number of daily tasks that need to be managed for the various customer centres
- very good format to the service reporting, clearly focused on the key service targets, with good tiering of details
- internal audit program for 2005 clearly based on risk and status of IT Service Management processes, with extra audits for higher risk processes

3.9.1   Improvement actions started on gaps found

In addition to small adjustments, it was decided that the Service Management tool should be replaced with a more automated one, to include an intelligent workflow engine. This new tool was implemented within a very short time (2 weeks), as all of the processes had already been developed and were operational.

3.9.2   Converting the result into profit

No financial calculations were made. One of the benefits achieved by the certification was the servicing of five banks on a high level (99.9% 7*24*365 availability) by almost the same number of staff as previously utilized for a single bank. This represents a saving of approximately 20 full-time employees when compared to the distributed operation.

The result was communicated via ING Group internal marketing and communications. As SCB is a shared service centre of ING Group N.V., only internal customers are serviced. No real marketing is considered useful. itSMF UK and certification body logos are utilized in any documents issued.

The key personnel involved in the certification were rewarded for their efforts with a bonus payment.

3.10 Preserving the certificate

This certificate is the basis for the continual improvement of SCB services.

As the organization is small, everyone is aware of the need to remain focused on quality and on opportunities for improvement. For this reason, further awareness improvement actions are not required.

As regards metrics and reviews, BS 15000 self assessment sheets are filled in on a yearly basis, with corrective actions initiated when gaps are identified.

Process owners have been assigned with the task of monitoring and improving compliance to the standard.

Monthly process review meetings are held to maintain the SIP and to address preventive and corrective actions. Internal audit generated items are also reviewed at these meetings.

3.10.1 Interim audits

Internal audits check the compliance status of all ISO 20000 processes. These audits take place twice a year and are the task of the internal auditor. The audit plan is based on the BS 15000 assessment questionnaire. Audit records are maintained, and corrective/preventive actions are initiated based on the findings. New SIP items are also initiated as required.

3.11 Project evaluation

The benefits, which were originally anticipated for the project, have been achieved. This was assisted by:
- full management commitment
- ITIL training of all staff
- assignment of process owners at an early phase
- tooling for:
  - process design (BWise)
  - Service Management (HP Openview Servicedesk)
  - process monitoring (HP Openview ServiceDesk Process Insight)
  - automated CMDB update

The main problematical issue was due to underestimating the importance of the Service Management tool. The originally selected, very simple and cheap tool was not performing well; it caused many non conformances in the execution of the service support processes, and also resulted in a lot of manual work. It has been replaced by a more advanced tool, which automates all workflows, prevents all deviations from the defined processes, automates CMDB updates and has a customer-web interface.

The introduction of service level management unexpectedly resulted in positive improvements. The relationship with customers (they are all within ING N. V.) improved a great deal; this was apparent from the feedback from our customer satisfaction surveys.

We learnt that we did not need to implement all of the content of the ITIL books, but that we could carefully select those practices that were essential or useful for our business. During the first year following certification we simplified many of the processes, which were sometimes overly complex, by removing over-detailed process steps.

3.11.1 Company message

ISO 20000 embeds the need for continual improvement, resulting in a more effective, efficient and controlled IT environment, in order to support the business and satisfy the customers. Achieving certification is not the end of the process, but merely the beginning of a new way of working. Having achieved ISO 20000 certification made it much easier to certify SCB for ISO 27001, as the basics of the information risk management process had been developed during the BS 15000 implementation project.

ISO 9001, which was achieved prior to BS 15000 and ISO 27001, was very useful when it came to creating a management system framework, as the requirements of all three of these standards are very similar.

For now, we have an integrated quality-, Service Management- and information risk management system, which covers all areas of our operation.

We believe that this is the best way to organize the activities of an IT service provider or an internal IT department.

Case 4:
Marval

CASE DETAILS	(anonymized company is allowed)
Company name	Marval
Country	United Kingdom
Year and Month of certification	BS 15000 - June 2005 ISO 20000 - February 2006
Certification body	DNV
Author of the case history	Manisha Champaneri
Role of author	IT Service Management and ISO 20000 Consultant
Company of author	Marval
Date of case logging	April 4, 2007

4.1   Organization type

Marval is a private held limited company, which was established in 1989.

4.1.1   Organizational size

The Marval Group consists of approximately 200 staff, located worldwide, in the UK, the Netherlands, Sweden, South Africa, Dubai, Singapore, Australia, Canada and the USA. This case study focuses on the UK office. Within the UK Service Desk, there are seven full time support staff. Overall they provide IT support worldwide, but for the scope of the certification the support is internally focused only.

4.1.2   Main activities

Marval supplies and supports our own in-house developed Service Management Software, with associated training in best practice and bespoke products. In addition, we also provide consultancy in the Service Management arena.

4.1.3   Relevance of IT Service Management

IT services is the core business proposition in an open market situation, for both internal and external customers; for this case study we will be focusing on the service provided internally. IT is indispensable for internal customers.

4.1.4   Customers

Marval delivers services to both internal and external customers. The Service Desk acts as third line support for Marval's Service Management Software for our external customers. For internal customers, the Service Desk delivers vital business support.

Internal customers are defined as employees of Marval Software and Marval Training and Consultancy. The UK Service Desk support internal customers, external customers (customers who have purchased the Marval tool) and partners.

4.2   Drivers for certification

As Marval continues to improve its products and services in IT Service Management to its global customers, it is equally dedicated to providing the best quality of IT Service Management within its own organization. Achieving ISO 20000 is just one step in reaffirming its commitment to best practice principles, and practicing what it preaches.

Our main driver for achieving certification was to improve the quality of both our internal and external support services. This was to make our services 'future proof'; in the future, customers will be increasingly more demanding. Other drivers included:
- staff not spending sufficient time on improvements
- a more competitive market place
- SLAs becoming the 'norm'
- teams finding it increasingly difficult to sell their success

Most of all, we wanted a first class Service Desk Team.

4.2.1 Main initiator
Marval's Management Team undertook a major initiative for its Service Delivery staff during 2005, initially to achieve BS 15000 and subsequently to attain ISO 20000 certification.

4.2.2 Business case
A formal business case was constructed, highlighting a high level cost model, together with current holding positions, KPIs and CSFs. The certification process was managed as a formal project with a dedicated Project Manager.

Benefits
Key Critical Success Factors identified included:
* strong leadership and management commitment
* reliance on teams to interact and realize their responsibilities to each other
* empowerment of process owners
* the need for a good ITSM tool to obtain evidence
* a requirement to slow down in order to speed up and improve
* concentration on 'Future Advantages' rather than on past disadvantages
* the fact that people will have loyalties, and may be sensitive to unnecessary criticism of existing methods
* involvement of everyone - especially of suspected 'problem staff'
* holding regular progress reviews
* development of a public relations process to sell the business and customer benefits

Costs
The main costs identified were time and resources. The journey to implement was made smoother by utilizing the company's own training and consultancy arm, Marval Training and Consultancy Ltd, who helped to oversee, guide and manage the process. Marval's own IT Service Management software tools helped to provide the process documentation and evidence required to achieve certification. In turn, expertise gained from the project allowed the Marval team to use the experience to help customers.

4.3 Quality management at the start of the project
When the project began, Marval used the BSI self assessment workbook to determine the current holding position. Matured and embedded processes existed for incident, problem, change and configuration, but not all processes were equally mature, and additional issues were highlighted:
* Existing processes and procedures did not always align; incident management had no relationship with problem management, yet both processes existed.
* Some processes did *not* exist, while others were not being used; release management was not followed, whereas service reporting was not used effectively for business decisions.
* There were resource related problems; staff still had to do their 'day job'; reviewing new processes and attending education programs needed to fit round 'business as usual' activities.
* Staff were reluctant to admit to a lack of knowledge or to limited understanding of requirements; because they were embarrassed to admit a lack of knowledge, subsequent educational material was of insufficient detail.

- Not everything was being recorded or measured, particularly performance and evidence of identified improvements; two minute jobs were not recorded, as support staff felt that it wasted time. Consequently, network outages were never recorded, as they lasted less than five minutes, and thus, no evidence was available on which to base improvements.
- Some improvement efforts suffered from 'scope creep'; as overall objectives of the improvement effort continued to grow, they threatened the achievement of the initial objectives.

4.3.1 IT Service Management methods established

IT Service Management was already embedded within Marval; for example, Marval required all members of staff be trained at ITIL Foundation level. The main focus of the new initiative was on moving towards a more prescriptive standard and on obtaining the evidence to prove it.

To re-enforce the staff re-orientation and mindset, Marval:
- explained Marval's Business Drivers for needing ISO 20000
- made team leaders accountable for their agreed deliverables
- removed any staff fears or suspicions, such as outsourcing or politics
- highlighted that they understood 'staff still have a day job'
- made clear that staff had a responsibility to their colleagues, their customers and the business to make it work
- informed the team that Regular Internal Audits were required
- set and agreed on an initial target date for the first audit

To re-enforce the critical role that the IT department plays within Marval, the company invested in:
- **training and education programs**:
  - ISO 20000 awareness for all teams
  - policy, process and procedures writing workshops (this helped 'buy-in' from the staff, by ensuring that they felt involved)
  - train/educate all staff in the agreed policies, processes and procedures
- **current 'holding' position** - the use of the self assessment workbook:
  - identified strengths, weaknesses and areas for improvement
  - identified process gaps and missing processes
- **IT Service Management technology**:
  - attaining ISO 20000 without a tool would have been resource intensive, difficult or even impossible
  - it was necessary to re-configure MSM tool classification processes and workflows to provide:
    - ◆ process control checks
    - ◆ evidence
    - ◆ reporting

4.4 Parties involved

Marval's Management Team initiated the ISO 20000 accreditation project, reinforcing that the company is committed to developing, maintaining and delivering quality IT services to its own staff in an effective and efficient way. This reflects its public commitment to quality IT Service Management, and the considerable work it does in this area with its external customers.

It also reflects the good, sound business sense of supporting internal customers and users to ensure that they have the tools they require to support the external customers upon whom the success of Marval depends. The Management Teams consisted of the two Managing Directors and a Project Manager who was also a consultant in the field. Updates throughout the project were highlighted in the monthly company meetings.

4.4.1   Management staff

Initially Management Team meetings took place to identify roles and responsibilities, and the importance of the project was also highlighted.

4.4.2   Employees

Employees were involved throughout the project. Marval scheduled workshops to help employees understand what the accreditation project entailed, how they could help and what the benefits were.

4.4.3   Customers

As well as the employees, customers were also involved throughout the project, via education workshops.

4.5   Initial assessment

Marval carried out an initial assessment. As well as assessments throughout the project using the self assessment workbook, the company also utilized the services of an external consultant: DNV spent a day advising the company as to both strengths and weaknesses.

DNV examined the company as though a formal audit was taking place, whilst advising Marval throughout. The scope of the assessment was the same as for a formal audit, with a complete assessment of all data.

The initial audit identified a general lack of evidence with which to backup the documentations (policies/processes/procedures). All changes require a back-out plan, yet there was no evidence of a back-out plan attached to the request. The existing documentation was more detailed than required. The auditor found that the tool was self explanatory, so there was no need to enter this into the documentation. This helped to reduce the pages per policy and process considerably.

Marval's policies, processes and procedures documents were too detailed for the scope of the accreditation. The auditor found that Marval's own tool (MSM) had most of the processes embedded in process workflows. This highlighted the need for less documentation. Overall the findings were positive, resulting in the company being ready for the formal audit once corrective actions had taken place. One of these corrective actions was to supply additional evidence that processes and procedures were being followed.

4.6   Decision to go for certification

The decision to seek certification was made in the beginning, see Section 4.2.

4.6.1   Scope
The scope was determined by the Management Team as follows:

> *"The delivery of managed internal IT service and systems to the UK-based organizations Marval Software Ltd and Marval Training and Consultancy Ltd."*

4.6.2   Objective
Marval's Service Management focus is on delivering the required services effectively, efficiently and economically:
- **effectively** - in that the required scale and quality of services to support the business processes will be available to business users
- **efficiently** - in terms of value for money
- **economically** - by delivering the required level of services within resource constraints

Service Management is expected to deliver according to the published and maintained performance measures agreed. The agreed performance targets for Service Management overall, and for individual processes or groups of processes, are promulgated to all staff.

Everyone involved in IT Service Management follows the requirements laid down in appropriate procedures and staff regulations. There are no exceptions to this rule, whether for senior managers or for staff performing only occasional roles within Service Management.

4.6.3   Organization
The project was run formally with a dedicated Project Manager. The Project Manager was initially a consultant assigned to the role. Throughout the project, staff were required to attend training, to participate in workshops and to help embed the signed-off documentation into the organization.

Internal resources were used throughout the project. As mentioned in Section 4.2, Marval used its own training and consultancy arm and IT Service Management software tools to smooth the journey towards the certification.

4.6.4   Funding
The project was carried out as 'business as usual'; therefore, no cash or specific budget was allocated to the project.

4.6.5   Action plan
A phased, parallel and practical approach was followed:
1. it was important *not* to under-estimate the education, people and cultural issues, and impact on delivery timeframes
2. policy, process, procedure and plans development and mapping was carried out in parallel
3. process development time frames may vary based on the current maturity level
4. time includes the period required for audits

4.6.6   Time plan
Table 4.1 shows the Time Plan.

Process	Time to implement
Marval tool re-alignment	14 days
Service Support	
Incident Management	1-2 months
Problem Management	1-2 months
Configuration Management	1-3 months
Change Management	1-2 months
Release Management	1 month
Service Delivery	
Service Level Management	1-2 months
Financial Management (Budgeting and Accounting for IT Services)	1-3 months`
Capacity Management	1-2 months
Business (Service) Continuity Management	1-3 months
Availability Management	1-2 months
Policies, processes and improvements plan alignment	
Policies and plans	1-2 months
Business Relationship Management and Supplier Management	1 month
Service Reporting	1 month
Information Security Management	1-2 months

Table 4.1   Time Plan

4.6.7   Communication plan
To ensure that plans were communicated effectively to all staff the company held:
- awareness workshops for all personnel
- education workshops for all personnel

4.7   Preparation for certification
The certification was prepared by the Project Manager, who took full control of the program, involving staff as and when required.

4.7.1   Selection of the certification agency
In order to select a certification agency, Marval sent out 'Requests for Tender' to Registered Certification Bodies (RCBs). Interviews took place to identify each auditors approach and to decide which one best fitted company requirements. The tender was sent out to four major RCBs, of which only two replied. The two RCBs were asked to attend Marval separately to answer key questions. As the standard was brand new, as well as being audited we wanted to go a step further and examine the ways in which the auditor could help us to exploit the standard to the maximum. As DNV were involved in the certification board, they had a good idea of what was required.

4.7.2   Collecting data on the management system
Evidence was collected through Marval's in-house tool, MSM.

4.7.3   Establish service improvement plan

Formal service improvement plans (SIPs) were created in a Word document, which was stored on the intranet for everyone to access. The identified SIPs were also logged in the Service Desk Tool. This enabled requests to be managed in an orderly fashion, with all relevant information recorded for evidence.

The service improvement plan was owned by the Service Desk at an operational level; this is the execution of the process. However, the Management Team, owned the creation and maintenance of the service improvement plan.

Measuring progress

Progress was measured in reports, such as trends analyses, and in emotional metrics, such as customer satisfaction surveys. This was to highlight the impact of the service improvements successes and failures, and to identify any additional SIP outcomes.

4.8   Formal audit

Under the terms of this case study, a 'formal audit' means that an external auditor (DNV) audited Marval for certification, while 'external audit' means auditing our external customers. In this case, no 'external audit' took place as the scope of the certificate was internal only. Certification was achieved for the internal services only.

4.8.1   Converting the result into profit

The result was communicated both internally and externally:
* through an internal company announcement
* via the Marval newsletter, which is distributed throughout the business, and to customers and partners
* a log was displayed on the company website
* a log was used on company sales literature
* via Marval presentations to the public, such as itSMF seminars

4.9   Preserving the certificate

In order to preserve the results, Marval undertake ongoing audits. The importance of ISO 20000 is highlighted at every company meeting. ISO 20000 is the first issue exposed to new staff and is embedded within everyone's job description and objectives. ISO 20000 education is delivered as and when required to staff; this was highlighted in the ongoing audits.

4.9.1   Awareness

Awareness workshops take place to highlight the importance of ISO 20000 within the organization. Key messages are relayed to new and current staff, emphasizing how they can help to maintain the certification.

4.9.2   Metrics and reviews

Many metrics are utilized in order to review service delivery and to identify potential improvements. These are fed into the CSIP (Table 4.2).

Process	Requirements
Service Level Management	Report on the number of SLAs in draft status (if applicable) and agreed
	Report on the number of SLAs and OLAs breaching agreed times
	Change Management reports on changes to SLAs - if applicable
	Highlight outcomes of SLAs from the above metrics with any supporting action plans
Service reporting	All SLA actual against targets ie highlighting SLA breaches, over engineered and under engineered SLAs
	Workload volumes reports or exception reports when volumes vary, ie Service Desk staff workloads
	Service Desk staff utilization compared to planned or project utilization
	Customer satisfaction survey results for solved closed
	Number and types of complaints
	Action plans outcomes from the service reports above
Service Continuity and Availability Management	Analysis of incident/problem management report regarding availability of service, plus actions plans
	IT Service Continuity Plan test results
	Report on recommended action plans for the above test
Financial management	Number of budgets produced on time
	Reports of expenditure against budget
	Standard financial reports, with actuals and targets and any relevant trends or variances
	Budget and costs, with variance for previous month and year to date
	Variation of actual spend against budget for each service
	Number of approved changes, by type, that record estimated costs
	Number and percentage of planned changes that input into the budget
	Number of service breaches caused by poor budgeting and cost tracking
Capacity Management	Measurement highlighting requests logged regarding capacity incidents/problems
	Customer, senior responsible owner and process owner sign-off of the predicted capacity and performance, based on expected changes - capacity plan

Table 4.2   Sample metrics for ISO 20000

4.9.3   Meeting structure on certification issues

Operational meetings take place on a daily basis; issues highlighted tend to be flagged with management for actions or recommendations.

4.9.4   Interim audits

Audits take place quarterly. Marval use the self assessment workbook as guidance on both non-conformance and conformance.

4.9.5   Preparation for re-assessment

Liaison takes place with the RCB regarding dates and agenda. Internally, checks take place at a very detailed level.

4.10 Evaluation of the business case

As the accreditation program was run as a formal project, the business case was also formally closed off once certification was achieved.

4.10.1 Actual benefits

The main actual benefit of accreditation has been that all requests are now logged, irrespective of their size. This helped with the SIP. Marval had real-life figures to work with, such as those involved in network outages with wireless networks; two seconds recorded down time could be equivalent to three hours when added together.

4.10.2 Real costs

No cost or budgets were allocated to the project.

4.11 Project evaluation

The project was challenging and an eye opener. Until an organization's service delivery is examined in detail, the company may have no idea of what is really going on. ISO 20000 allowed the Service Desk to be audited, using an internationally recognized standard. The entire project was overwhelming; Marval is the first company in the UK to gain certification, so it was difficult to predict the final outcome.

Key Critical Success Factors were:
- strong leadership and management commitment
- reliance on teams to interact and realize their responsibilities to each other
- empowerment of process owners
- the need for a good ITSM tool to obtain evidence
- a requirement to slow down in order to speed up and improve
- concentration on 'Future Advantages' rather than on past disadvantages
- the fact that people will have loyalties, and may be sensitive to unnecessary criticism of existing methods
- involvement of everyone - especially the suspected 'problem staff'
- holding regular progress reviews
- development of a public relations process to sell the business and customer benefits

Staff 'buy-ins' are a key issue; staff were reluctant to become involved, as they were unable to see the benefits of the certification. Unfortunately, as the standard was brand new, management had no examples of other organizations who had achieved the certification. However, it did present an advantage, by allowing the company to become involved in the development of the standard, and thus providing a more in-depth view of why the standard was initially developed. This was ultimately utilized to assist with staff 'buy-in'.

The main concerns when implementing ISO 20000 are people, people and people … they are key to the success, and crucial to the certification. ISO 20000 is a process based standard, but it still requires people to follow the processes. Staff involvement is the key concern for a company when implementing ISO 20000.

4.11.1 Company special message

"ISO 20000 has greatly improved Marval's overall performance, communication and attitude to service quality and continual improvement."

"We believe that ISO 20000 should be obligatory for every Service Department and 3rd party supplier."

"Do not go for ISO 20000 until your team can put their hands on their hearts and say … 'we are confident in our ability to be audited'."

Case 5:
NCS Pte Ltd, Singapore

CASE DETAILS	(anonymized company is allowed)
Company name	NCS Pte Ltd
Country	Singapore
Year and Month of certification	2005, December
Certification body	TÜV SÜD PSB Certification Pte Ltd
Authors of the case history	Foo Nian Chou Chew Hwee Hong Christiane Chung Ah Pong
Role of authors	Foo Nian Chou, *Chief (IMS, Infrastructure Management and Solutions)* Chew Hwee Hong, *Senior Manager (PQM, Process & Quality Management)* Christiane Chung Ah Pong, *Lead Consultant (PQM, Process & Quality Management)*
Company of author	NCS Pte Ltd
Date of case logging	April - August 2007

5.1   Organization type

NCS Group is an information technology (IT) and communications engineering services provider, operating in ten countries and 14 cities in the Asia Pacific and Middle East regions. Its headquarters are in Singapore and it is a wholly-owned subsidiary of the SingTel Group.

Company name	NCS PTE. LTD.
Address	5 Ang Mo Kio Street 62 NCS Hub Singapore 569141
Type of company	Private Limited
Nature of establishment	Information technology and communications engineering solutions provider
Areas of specialisation	Consulting services, business solutions, infrastructure management and solutions, technology solutions

Table 5.1   Outline information on NCS

Today, the NCS Group has offices in Australia (Sydney), China (Beijing, Chengdu, Guangzhou, Shanghai and Suzhou), Hong Kong SAR, India, Korea, Malaysia, the Middle East (Bahrain), Singapore, Sri Lanka and the Philippines. It also serves customers in Brunei, Fiji, Indonesia, Kuwait, Kyrgyzstan, Mauritius, Pakistan, Qatar, Thailand and Victoria, South Australia.

NCS's wholly-owned subsidiaries are:
- NCS Information Technology (Suzhou) Co Ltd
- NCSI Holdings Pte Ltd
- NCSI (India) Pte Ltd
- NCSI (HK) Limited
- NCSI Holdings (Malaysia) Sdn Bhd
- NCSI (Malaysia) Sdn Bhd
- NCSI (Australia) Pty Limited
- NCS Communications Engineering Pte Ltd
- NCSI (Lanka) Ptv Ltd
- NCSI Philippines, Inc
- NCSI (Korea) Co Limited
- NCSI (ME) W L L
- NCSI (Shanghai) Co Ltd

NCS industry achievements include:
- Gartner Dataquest (Aug 2005) ranked NCS 1st in Singapore and 10th in Asia-Pacific (excluding Japan) in Professional Services.
- IDC ranked NCS 1st in Singapore and 15th in Asia-Pacific (excluding Japan) in IT Services for 2004. Gartner ranked NCS as 1st in Singapore and 11th in Asia Pacific on market share for Professional Services for 2005.
- NCS is ranked 41th on the International Association of Outsourcing Professionals (IAOP) Global Outsourcing 100 List.

- NCS is Asia-Pacific Top 15 IT Vendor, 2005 by Strategic 100, MIS.
- NCS is the Singapore Government's top IT contractor for FY2005 and FY2004.

5.1.1 Organizational size

The NCS group is 4,000 people strong, of which some 20% are located outside Singapore. We are committed to providing our customers with the highest levels of service. We have produced the largest pool of Certified IT Project Managers (awarded by the Singapore Computer Society) in Singapore.

5.1.2 Main activities

NCS provides a one-stop, end-to-end suite of IT and communications engineering solutions to meet customers' business and technology needs. We have in-depth domain knowledge and unique delivery capabilities, which focus on defining, realizing and sustaining business values for our customers, via the innovative use of technology. Our main service lines are:

- **Consulting services** - NCS offers consulting services in business continuity, e-Government, strategic organization, IT Service Management and IT applications and infrastructure. We particularly aim at thought leadership, industry best practices, deep domain knowledge and technology expertise. We synchronize and fuse business strategies and technologies, to help our customers capitalize on the rapidly changing landscape of business opportunities and technological advancement.
- **Business solutions** - NCS' business solutions include business process outsourcing, business process re-engineering, application design, development, implementation and maintenance, ERP implementation and maintenance, and systems integration.
- **Infrastructure management and solutions** - NCS infrastructure management and solutions aim to free customers to focus on their core business activities. We ensure that as our customers' businesses grow, the IT systems, which are needed to support this growth, develop in parallel. NCS offers a suite of infrastructure management and solutions including data centre hosting and operations services, managed network and security services, client platforms services, enterprise systems management services, facility management services and business continuity services. Our Data Centre, amongst the largest in ASEAN, is fully equipped with round-the-clock staffing by our IT professionals, and its services are ISO 27001 certified. NCS is also one of the seven companies certified in Business Continuity and Disaster Recovery by Infocomm Development Authority (IDA) and IT Standard Committee of Singapore. In December 2005, TÜV SÜD PSB Certification Pte Ltd awarded NCS with BS 15000 certification, and the surveillance audit conducted in February 2007 was successfully completed against ISO/IEC20000.
- **Technology solutions** - The NCS technology solutions capability, with over 50 years of in-depth knowledge and experience, differentiates NCS from other IT companies. It effectively integrates IT and engineering expertise into one business solution. Our technology solutions include engineering and radio communication comprising of smart security solutions, transportation solutions, intelligent solutions and C4ISR (command, control, communication, computer, intelligence, surveillance and reconnaissance), IT infrastructure systems, IT security training and certification, and telecommunication and multimedia.

5.1.3 Relevance of IT Service Management

NCS Group is an information technology (IT) and communications engineering services provider to both commercial and government organizations; IT Service Management is part of our core business, and it is key to service delivery to our valued customers.

We manage mission critical and multi-platform projects in industries which include the public sector, education, financial services and insurance, healthcare and life sciences, homeland security, logistics and manufacturing, telecoms and utilities, and transportation, where IT and Service Management are indispensable.

5.1.4 Customers

The case study concerns NCS as a service provider in an open market with external customers. NCS' portfolio of blue chip customers testifies to the company's strong track record spanning companies and governments in the Asia Pacific region. Major customers include Citibank Asia Pacific Technology Group, Standard Chartered Bank, Prudential, DBS Bank, Maybank, Shanghai National Accounting Institute, Hi-P (China) Electronics, Singapore Airlines, the Hong Kong SAR Government, the Singapore Government Ministries and Statutory Boards, the Mauritius Government, the Kuwaiti Government, the Sri Lankan Government, the Thai Government, Institutes of Higher Learning in Singapore, Singapore Management University, SingTel Group, Honda Diracc, BP, Awal Hoteling, Lafarge Asia Pacific and Optus.

5.2 Drivers for certification

The key drivers for certification were to provide NCS with a competitive edge over our competitors in the outsourcing market. ISO 20000 was set to become a basic tender requirement for service providers. We aimed to adopt the ITIL framework to deliver clear roles and responsibilities, and standard practices and standard deliverables, to produce consistent, scalable and reliable value for money services to our customers. The ISO 20000 certification will allow us to benchmark ourselves against best practices. It will also provide clarity to both the outsourcer and the service provider for better alignment of expectations on service quality.

NCS also embarked on the ISO 20000 certification for its potential external marketing and commercial benefits. It provided a means by which to benchmark our service delivery, against an international standard for Service Management, which is part of our core business.

Besides providing us with a competitive edge, NCS aimed at operational benefits by improving our service reliability and consistency. It also provides a visible commitment to managing the provision of IT services to our customers.

5.2.1 Main initiator

The Management of *Infrastructure Management and Solutions* in consultation with the *Process and Quality Management group* and key *Service Delivery Directors* initiated the certification project in 2004.

5.2.2   Business case

Return on investment (ROI) identified in the business case included:

- an increase of about 15% in business, from customers requesting an ITSM service standard
- a reduction in costs of 20% (eg due to reduction in rework, better managed risks, etc.)
- improved staff mobility in the longer term, given consistent ITSM practices

5.2.2.1 Benefits

Overall, ISO 20000 provides a recognized and proven management system that allows NCS to plan, deliver, monitor, review and improve services. The standard not only looks at operational aspects, but also focuses on the business controls covering associated risks. Some of the general benefits identified include:

- a formal framework for our service delivery
- benchmarking our processes against best practices
- enhancing our company reputation, which will further improve NCS's leading market position
- improved customer satisfaction and customer loyalty
- a competitive advantage, through consistent, cost-effective and scalable services

Various stake-holders' interests (namely NCS, our customers and our employees) were considered. ISO 20000 provides NCS with a framework addressing a number of governance measures, thereby providing better management of risks and better profitability. It provides us with a means to deliver consistent and reliable services to our customers.

By embarking on the certification and by adopting the ISO 20000 framework, we aimed at aligning with our customer's expectations, and providing clarity, with a better visibility and control of the performance of the various outsourced services, through constant planning, reporting and communication: for example, by service reviews and reporting, escalation of major incidents and by involving the customers in change management.

We considered employee satisfaction and staff retention as another area. Through the standard alignment and process, staff would be equipped with new skill sets, which would add to their career and competency development.

We also identified other operational benefits:

- new roles and responsibilities were defined during the ISO 20000 implementation; these have provided clear accountabilities in our service delivery
- mature processes, which are repeatable, consistent and self-improving
- ISO 20000 has provided a more structured framework for pro-activeness; adopting a proactive approach (eg problem management, investigating the root causes of both actual and potential incidents) has reduced operational overhead costs, as preventive measures are identified to avoid repeated or potential incidents
- continual improvement is institutionalized, with targets for improvement in areas of quality, costs and resource utilization
- consistency in delivery is enforced through the deployment of an ITSM tool for service support processes

For management, ISO 20000 provides a framework to a number of governance measures, thereby providing better management of risks. It provides management with a better visibility of the service performance via regular service reporting and review of metrics, and allows management to make informed decisions.

As for business benefits, certification to ISO 20000 can help demonstrate that the customer is the key focus within NCS IT service delivery. We are able to adopt technology in a more systematic way to meet the business and customer needs.

5.2.2.2 Costs

NCS management viewed the initial costs, required in order to deploy ITSM, as an investment with long-term returns. Both internal and external costs were identified. **Internal costs** had to address the three specific areas of people, tool and process definition and deployment:

- **People** - at organizational level, a percentage of the corporate budget is allocated for staff training; for the IMS group, the relevant staff are scheduled to attend ITIL related courses; internal training on NCS ITSM processes is also conducted on a regular basis
- **Tool** - NCS recognized that an ITSM tool (with the associated hardware and licences) had to be purchased; resources had to be provided, to evaluate ITSM tools and to customize the selected tool
- **Process definition and deployment** - this includes the effort required to define, review and approve the processes and to deploy them to the project teams; see Section 5.4 for further details on the structure and staff involvement

External costs identified included the cost of engaging an external consultant to do a current state assessment and a readiness check, and the costs of engaging an RCB (Registered Certification Body) to conduct the formal audit.

5.3   Quality management at the start of the project

At the start of the project, a quality management system was already in place. NCS achieved ISO 9001 certification in 1997. To achieve our vision to be a world-class company in the global market, NCS then looked beyond ISO 9001. In 1998, NCS officially adopted the business excellence model, the Singapore Quality Award (SQA) framework, to drive excellence in all aspects of the organization. NCS attained Singapore Quality Class (SQC) status in July 1999, and the People Developer Award (PDA) in March 2000.

In 2003, NCS was the first company in Singapore to attain CMMI Maturity level 3; in April 2006, we attained CMMI Maturity level 5 for NCS IT Suzhou in China. We attained CMMI Maturity level 5 for NCS Singapore in July 2007.

The NCS Data Centre (Singapore) was BS 7799 certified in October 2003, following a competent and independent assessment. The conversion to ISO 27001 was successfully completed in July 2007.

In December 2004, NCS was awarded the SS 507 certification as a Business Continuity and Disaster Recovery provider. SS 507 is a standard for Business Continuity (BC)/Disaster Recovery (DR) Service Providers. It is developed by the Infocomm Development Authority (IDA) and the IT Standards Committee (ITSC) of Singapore. The requirements benchmark against the top practices in the region, and stipulate the operating, monitoring and upkeep of the BC/DR services offered.

5.4   Parties involved

A team comprised of NCS internal staff was formed to drive the initiative. The team included senior management, project teams and the *Process & Quality Management* team, as shown in the Deployment Organization Structure in Figure 5.1.

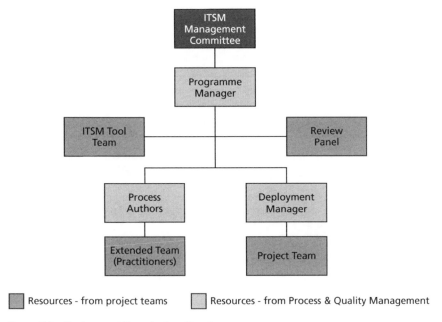

Figure 5.1   Deployment Organization Structure

5.4.1   Management staff

NCS management is represented by the ITSM Management Committee and the Program Manager in the deployment structure (Figure 5.1). The ITSM Management Committee (ITSM MC) comprised the Chief of IMS and Service Delivery Directors. All were involved from the beginning of the project, and throughout the certification journey.

The key responsibilities included:
- setting direction for ITIL alignment and BS 15000 certification
- providing sponsorship for the program, by ensuring that resources were committed and available for the project
- endorsing the implementation approach (ITSM process definition and deployment)

The Program Manager was the head of the *Process and Quality Management* group with responsibility for:
- defining the implementation approach and deployment plan
- monitoring and tracking the overall program progress
- provide fortnightly updates to the ITSM Management Committee
- highlighting any major issues, and proposing problem resolution to the ITSM Management Committee

5.4.2　Employees

Staff from the respective departments were involved from the beginning of the project. The objectives of the project were communicated to them, and they were kept continuously updated on the progress of the project via emails and team meetings.

Groups involved included:
- **Review Panel** - various subject matter experts with responsibility for:
  - final review and approval of processes
  - providing guidance and consultancy to the process team on process definition
- **ITSM tool group** - three individuals, who:
  - evaluated and proposed a suitable ITSM tool
  - defined the tool deployment schedule, outlining the key milestones
  - organized the overall tool deployment
  - conducted training on the ITSM tool for the project teams
- **process authors** - two people for the first six months, with an additional four people on a part-time basis as the *extended team*, responsible for:
  - the overall completion of the process
  - updating the Program Manager on the progress
  - co-ordinating the submission of the final draft to the Review Panel for approval
  - definition of process documents including checklist, templates and guidelines
  - seeking input from the extended team on the draft process, consolidating and reviewing feedback
- **Extended team** - ITIL trained practitioners, to:
  - provide feedback on the process contents and applicability
  - provide samples of good guidelines and checklists
  - act as consultants to the process authors
- **Deployment Managers** - coming from the *Process and Quality Management* Group, on a part-time basis (1/2 headcount) per project and responsible for:
  - the overall deployment of ITSM processes to project teams
  - developing and executing the deployment plan

- Responsibilities were assigned to the **Project Team**, to:
  - familiarize themselves with respective ITSM processes, metrics required
  - gather metrics from processes to baseline process performance
  - implement and comply to ITSM process standards
  - provide regular process updates to the Deployment Manager

The ITSM Management Committee, the Program Manager and the Review Panel comprised of a total of about ten people.

The various groups were trained in ITIL Foundation, on NCS ITSM processes and on the ITSM tool.

5.4.3 Customers

NCS engaged the relevant customers by briefing them on ITIL practices, creating awareness and promoting ITSM concepts, to get their buy-in and commitment to work on the project. Regular meetings were held to keep the customers informed on progress and to gather their inputs on interfacing areas. Items discussed included timeframe, deployment approach and process interfaces between NCS and the customer.

Incident Management is an example of one of the processes which interfaced with the customers (confirming the parties to be notified in the event of major incidents and the frequency of escalation to the customers). Change Management is another process where customers were involved (for example, in the change approval workflow). A third area discussed regularly with our customers was that of Service improvement initiatives through the Service Improvement Plan (SIP).

After successful certification, we shared lessons learnt and audit findings with our customer base.

5.4.4 Subcontractors

There was no specific alignment required by external subcontractors, as existing practice,s such as monitoring and reviewing suppliers' performance, were in place.

However, internal service providers, such as the helpdesk, were involved throughout the project and were kept up-to-date on a regular basis via email and meetings.

5.4.5 Third parties

NCS participated in the Singapore itSMF conference in 2006, to share its experience on the BS 15000 certification journey. In June 2007, NCS discussed implementing ITSM at the 'Annual Singapore Data Centre Dynamics Conference', a global Data Centre networking and knowledge exchange conference for mission critical facilities and IT infrastructure. In August 2007, one of our Service Delivery Directors was a speaker at the 'ITIL V3 Asia Pacific Summit - Singapore' on 'The practical experience of implementing ITIL'. We also continue to discuss our ITSM approach and our experience, with potential customers, to create awareness and to promote ITSM concepts.

5.5   Initial assessment

In late 2004, when NCS embarked on the initiative, as BS 15000 was a new standard in Singapore and no organization was, as yet, certified to it, NCS's management took the decision to engage a third party consultant to perform a current state assessment and a readiness check. Based on the gaps identified, the NCS teams brainstormed on the best and most effective way to address and close the gaps, prior to the external audit by TÜV SÜD PSB Certification Pte Ltd in October 2005.

The *Process & Quality Management* team subsequently developed its own internal audit checklists based on the experience gained by working with the external consultants and through the external audit by TÜV SÜD PSB Certification Pte Ltd. After the certification was completed, NCS used its own checklists in subsequent internal audits.

The scope of the current state assessment outsourced to the external party was the same as that on which NCS was seeking certification (see Section 5.6.1). The assessment by the third party was done in five stages, from March to August 2005:

- **Stage 1 (March 2005)** - involved discussion and agreement on the scope for certification, and the roles and responsibilities of the external consultant and NCS
- **Stage 2 (March 2005)** - involved document collation, inspection and analysis by the external consultant
- **Stage 3 (April 2005)** - included on-site interviews with key staff to verify practice and adherence areas
- **Stage 4 (April 2005)** - involved the inspection of systems environment, architecture design and supporting ITSM tools; subsequently, the consultant produced a gap analysis report, highlighting the gaps by process areas; NCS's teams worked on the corrective actions to address the gaps identified
- **Stage 5 (August 2005)** - the external consultant verified that the gaps identified in earlier stages were addressed, and performed a readiness check

The gap analysis report produced at the end of Stage 4 used a rating scale of 1 to 5 to indicate the maturity level of our processes, with 1 being the lowest maturity and 5 being at an optimized level meeting all the requirements of the BS 15000 standard.

Wider gaps were identified in some processes such as Problem, Configuration and Availability Management, whilst other processes such as Security, Service Continuity and Financial Management were of a higher maturity state.

The analysis report was used as input to define the alignment plan for the BS 15000 standard, along with a detailed project plan and schedule.

Stage 5 saw all the processes reaching the maturity level, which the external consultant assessed as ready for external certification.

5.6   Decision to go for certification

Stage 5 of the readiness check exercise concluded on a positive note with the external consultant's recommendation for NCS to proceed with the external certification. The report presented to NCS's teams highlighted that "there were significant improvements made over the past four months towards compliance to the BS 15000 Standard specifications. The work done is truly a demonstration of NCS' core values in action. We congratulate everyone involved in accomplishing so much, in such a short time."

NCS teams comprising of the IMS's Management, the *Process & Quality Management* group and the operations teams reached a common consensus to proceed with the external certification.

5.6.1   Scope

As BS 15000 was a new standard in the Singapore market when NCS embarked on the initiative, NCS adopted a phased approach. At first, the focus of the certification was on those services where NCS had clear management control of the processes.

This focus included:
- provision of Mainframe Data Centre Services
- provision of Wide Area Network Connectivity Services and Remote Access Infrastructure Services to the Singapore Government

There was an appendix to the certificate, stating:

The scope of certification covers the following services at NCS Hub:
- Data Centre Facilities Services
- Operations Management Services
- System Management Services
- Database Management Services
- Business Continuity Services
- Project Management Services
- Managed Security Services
- Managed Network Services
- Service Desk Services
- Customer Services

These were successfully audited in October 2005, with the award of the certificate in December 2005. However, NCS worked on an expansion of the scope to other services, and in January/February 2007, during the surveillance audit, the scope was expanded to our Internet Data Centre Services and Infrastructure Management Services for a client's data centre. The new scope included:
- provision of Data Centre Services
- provision of Wide Area Network Connectivity Services and Remote Access Infrastructure Services to the Singapore Government
- provision of Infrastructure Management Services for MediNet

The services being certified were operated from Singapore, the location for the certification was based on this location.

5.6.2 Objective
The objectives of the project were to be certified to reap the benefits outlined during the project initiation, as outlined in Section 5.2.2.

5.6.3 Funding
The project was internally funded by the *Infrastructure Management and Solutions* (IMS) group.

5.6.4 Action plan
The initiative was managed as a project with a Program Manager assigned to define, monitor and review the schedule against planned activities. NCS adopted the steps defined in the ITIL version 2 book on 'Planning to Implement Service Management'[1], as shown by Figure 5.2.

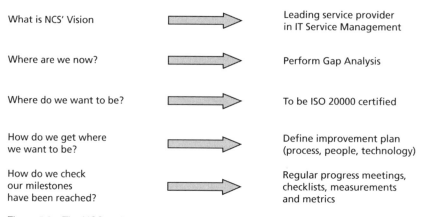

Figure 5.2   The NCS action plan

5.6.5 Time plan
The certification initiative started in September 2004 and the external audit was conducted in October 2005, with the certification awarded in December 2005. The key milestones are summarized below, together with the elapsed time required (in parentheses):
- definition, review and approval of policies, processes and relevant procedures (four months)
- training of staff on the defined policies, processes and procedures (two months)
- closing of gaps and deployment of practices (six months)
- ITSM tool evaluation, selection, purchase, customization and training of staff (six months)
- collection of at least three months data prior to audit

Some of these activities were carried out in parallel.

---

1 ITIL version 3 presents this model as the 'Continual Service Improvement model' in its book on Continual Service Improvement (CSI).

5.6.6 Communication plan

Regular communication took place at a variety of levels throughout the project. Through the regular ITSM MC meetings, there was communication from the Chief of IMS to his next level, the Service Delivery Directors (SDDs), on his directions and plans. There were regular reviews of the progress of the project and on the issues faced by the team. The SDDs acted as the linchpins of the group, between the Chief and their next level managers, who, in turn, would disseminate the information to their teams during their regular team meetings or via emails.

Similarly, the ITSM MC meetings provided the platform for both the *Process and Quality Management* team and the ITSM tool group to provide their updates. The *Process and Quality Management* team provided updates on process enhancements and releases, whilst the ITSM tool group updated on the ITSM tool evaluation, tool customization and deployment.

5.7 Preparation for certification

The certification journey was given significant importance, and managed as a key project, with a Program Manager assigned to track, monitor and report on the progress. Fortnightly meetings were held with the IMS's chief, to provide updates and to discuss issues encountered.

5.7.1 Selection of the certification agency

As TÜV SÜD PSB Certification Pte Ltd is the certification agency which NCS engaged for ISO 9001 and BS 7799 audits, it was a logical choice to select them as the agency for the ISO 20000 certification.

5.7.2 Determine scope with certification agency

NCS drafted the proposed scope based on the scoping guidelines available at www.bs15000certification.com[2] and discussed it with the certification agency. The latter requested the organization chart, to ascertain its understanding of the location boundaries and the services to be encompassed in the audit scope. After a few discussions with NCS, the certification body recommended some fine-tuning to remove ambiguities.

It is important to note that the initial proposed scoping statement was done from NCS's perspective based on its objectives of certification with reference to its line of business. It had been based on NCS IMS's organization chart, which did not reflect the services and scope in a meaningful way to external parties. This illustrates the importance of engaging the certification body as early as possible in the certification journey, to seek its inputs on the scoping statement.

5.7.3 Collecting data on the management system

The metrics required for the service support processes (incident, problem, change, configuration and release) are generated from the ITSM tool whilst the metrics for service delivery processes are generated from monitoring tools. Examples of incident management metrics include:
* number of incidents logged in period
* number of incidents closed in period
* number of outstanding incidents as at end of period
* number and percentage of incidents resolved within SLA

---

2 Now www.isoiec20000certification.com.

Metrics from the other processes are similar in nature, to help the process managers gauge the health status of the process. The various process managers collated and reviewed the metrics on a monthly basis. They performed trend analysis on the metrics, identified areas for improvement, recorded any actions for improvement and provided these as inputs to the Service Improvement Plan (SIP). The SIP and any non conformances were reviewed with the ITSM Management Committee on a quarterly basis.

5.7.4   Establish service improvement plan

Various areas of improvements were identified by each project, taking into account directions and ROI set by the management under the business case (Section 5.2.2). For each area, a baseline was set and corresponding targets (eg in areas of quality, costs or utilization) and timeframe for improvement were established. The SIP covered areas of improvement in operations, process integration and enhancements, staff training, ITSM tool, deployment, etc.

For example, as one of the ROIs identified was a reduction in rework, one of the teams observed that there was a high number of operation errors in handling a particular system, which resulted in rework. The service owner logged this as an improvement item in the SIP with a target of zero errors. A SIP action plan was defined to address this, and the number of errors was brought down to zero after six months, resulting in improvement in operational efficiency and cost savings.

Respective line managers own the respective SIPs of their projects. The progress and status of the SIP is reviewed by line managers in their monthly Service Management meetings.

5.8   Internal audit

The NCS Process and Quality Management group developed its own internal audit checklists which were used in internal audits. As in other internal audits (eg for ISO 9001), audit schedules were planned and auditees were kept informed on the audit schedule and on the scope of audits. Audit findings were logged and audit reports were provided to the auditees in order for them to address the findings. A summary report highlighting the key findings was also provided to the IMS Management.

Most gaps identified internally were tracked, with respective owners putting in place corrective and preventive actions (eg in SIP) to address the findings prior to external certification.

5.9   External audit

The external audit was conducted on 13-14th October 2005 by three auditors from TÜV SÜD PSB Certification Pte Ltd. There were no surprises, as no major non conformances were found, and the audit closed with NCS being recommended for certification subject to successful clearance of the audit findings by the RCB. The certificate was awarded in December 2005.

5.9.1 Gaps found
The categories of the audit findings used by the certification agency are:
- **Category 1 findings** - major non conformances
- **Category 2 findings** - minor non conformances
- **AFI** - areas for Improvement

As there were no Category 1 findings, NCS was recommended for the certification, subject to submission of evidence of corrective actions taken within a month of the audit.

Some of these were not found in the initial assessment conducted by the external consultants as audit is a sampling process. Internal audit or assessment does not guarantee that all non conformances are uncovered.

5.9.2 Improvement actions started on these gaps
The audit guides from the Process and Quality Management group discussed the findings with the auditees, and identified the root cause, corrective and preventive actions. These were documented, recorded and tracked until closure. Improvements were implemented in the areas of deployment, processes and tools.

Under Service Continuity Management, one of the findings was that "there is no objective evidence that the Service Continuity Service Plan gets its inputs from the Business Plan". The practice of getting inputs from the Business Plan was, however, in place. Participation in planning sessions and questions related to the Business Plan were already in place in the Review of Business Impact Analysis Form. But this practice was not explicitly formalized in the Business Continuity Plan, and this was identified as the root cause of the issue. The corrective action taken was to have the team make a statement in the Business Continuity Plan, which stated that inputs have been taken from the relevant Business Plans.

5.9.3 Converting the result into profit
There were multiple announcements and expressions of thanks, by various levels of management to staff, upon the award of the certificate. A lunch party was organized to reward staff for their hard work and for making NCS the first organization in Singapore to achieve the BS 15000 certification.

Customers were kept informed, and marketing materials (with the itSMF UK logo, where appropriate) were updated, to reflect this significant milestone in our quality journey. Marketing materials are published on NCS's intranet, as well as being printed in brochures and posters. At customers' requests, we have shared our experience of the certification journey as part of our awareness program.

Our strategic technology partners, such as Alcatel, BMC, Computer Associates, CISCO, EMC, F5 Networks, Hewlett Packard, Microsoft and Sun Microsystems collaborated to congratulate NCS on this major milestone, in a congratulatory advertisement which appeared in a local newspaper, 'Business Times', in April 2006.

NCS is also listed under the ISO/IEC website as a certified organization in Singapore.

5.10 Preserving the certificate

Achieving ISO 20000 certification is not a destination, but a continuous journey.

5.10.1 Awareness

There is regular in-house training to constantly reinforce the message of the NCS's Service Management objectives. The ITSM MC continues to meet on a regular basis to maintain the momentum.

5.10.2 Metrics and reviews

An NCS Audit Program Manager, under the Process and Quality Management Department, is responsible for planning the Internal Quality Audit (IQA) and the external surveillance audit master plan, on an annual basis. He monitors the progress of the IQA and the surveillance program, carries out the half-yearly analysis of the program, and recommends process improvement opportunities.

KPIs of the IQA include that:
• planning the IQA cycle and submission for approval are to be done at least four weeks prior to the start of the field audit
• an IQA detailed findings report is to be sent within one week following the completion of the field audit, to auditee management and auditee
• corrective and preventive actions should be completed within three months from the date when the action plan was constituted

5.10.3 Agreements with line- and process management

Internal audits and surveillance audits are centrally managed and co-ordinated by the NCS Audit Program Manager, with inputs and approval from the IMS Management. The lead auditor will analyze and highlight key audit findings and recommendations to IMS Line Managers for them to follow-up.

5.11 Evaluation of the business case

As we have just implemented ITSM for a few pilot projects and services, it is too early to conclude as to whether we have achieved the quantitative gains which were defined in the business case. However, there has been an upward trend from outsourcers requiring ITSM, and NCS has been able to respond confidently to these requirements.

As regards reduction in rework, service owners have experienced an increase in operational efficiency, with the spirit of continual service improvement managed through SIPs.

We have also observed that staff working in the pilot projects and services have internalized ITSM practices (supported by the same ITSM tool), and they now speak in a common language, using ITIL terminology. We are confident that when ITSM practices are extended to cover further projects, staff mobility will be greatly improved. This is illustrated by the way in which some of the process managers from the first certification projects easily took on similar roles in subsequent programs.

5.11.1 Actual benefits

Benefits derived from this project include:

- systematic identification and review of service improvements
- consistent practices and service delivery
- better visibility and control of service delivery, with regular reviews of metrics
- a more competitive edge when responding to tenders, with an ability to show compliance to a leading worldwide standard

5.11.2 Real costs

The project teams initially experienced an additional 10-20% increase in their workload, due to the learning curve of new processes and the ITSM tool. These were not factored in the initial planning. However, after the deployment, the practices were institutionalized, and we recognize that it was worth investing in the initial additional effort in order to reap long-term benefits. Other resources (eg from the Process & Quality Management group, ITSM tool group, etc.) were as budgeted.

5.11.3 Ultimate appraisal of the business case

There has been a high level of satisfaction at all levels: management, staff and customer. Customers have appreciated the work, and have experienced improvement in service delivery. NCS internal service owners have better visibility of their service performance and a framework for the management of their services. Staff are proud of what has been achieved, and there is an overall sense of achievement throughout the organization.

5.12 Project evaluation

As BS 15000/ISO 20000 was a new standard when we embarked on this project in 2004, it was a challenge to understand the exact meaning of certain clauses within the standard and the aims of implementation. In order to address this, key drivers attended the BS 15000 Lead Auditor and Consultant course, to equip themselves with the right skill sets.

One of the key concerns was how the project teams would maintain 'business as usual' whilst embracing new practices under ITSM. This was addressed by using resources from support teams such as the *Process & Quality Management* Team and the ITSM tool group, and by defining a realistic schedule for staff adjustment.

There were concerns that staff would be resistant to change. In order to address this, clear directions and targets were set by the chief in the IMS Strategy Plan. IMS briefings were conducted, to provide general information and to raise awareness of the benefits that would be realized by implementing ITSM.

We applied project management principles to organize the certification journey, with focus on deliverables, schedule and timeline, addressing three key components: People, Tool and Processes. We had a well-planned deployment roadmap, with associated objectives and dedicated resources.

The 'People' issue was the key obstacle. New processes and procedures were introduced, together with an ITSM tool. This resulted in changes to the way in which operations had to be carried out. However, there was initial resistance from project teams in adopting the new processes and the ITSM tool. The tool was blamed for problems. We recognized that a successful ITSM implementation required everyone to have common goals, objectives and to move in the same direction.

In order to address the problems, with the IMS's Management support, the *Process and Quality Management* group, together with the Service Delivery Directors, were the designated 'ITSM Champions', to convert ITSM non-believers into ITSM supporters by re-enforcing the benefits which ITSM brings to staff. Ongoing education, training and persistence were provided to educate staff on ITSM processes and on the usage of the ITSM tool to drive consistency.

This resulted in enormous team spirit, passion and high commitment from all staff involved, with strong support from the management. The 'ITSM Champions' drove the implementation and maintained momentum.

Existing processes already used for ISO 9001 and BS 7799 were utilized. We adopted and adapted from ITIL to cater to NCS's unique requirements.

Although the process was not always easy, it is something that the company would choose to repeat.

5.12.1 Company message
Our 'golden rules for achieving ISO 20000 certification' are:
- to have a vision and to communicate that vision
- to ensure that senior management and all staff buy-in to the initiative; this is a key aspect successful implementation
- to have a formal structure or a committee to drive and manage the change
- to communicate and engage the staff, customers and suppliers on a regular basis to maintain momentum
- to plan the deliverables with a realistic schedule; it is not an overnight project
- to create a sense of urgency and motivation
- to empower and engage others
- to consolidate and institutionalize improvements

Case 6:

Nippon Securities Technology Co., Ltd, Japan

CASE DETAILS	(anonymized company is allowed)
Company name	Nippon Securities Technology Co Ltd
Country	Japan
Year and Month of certification	July 17, 2006
Certification body	DNV certification Ltd
Authors of the case history	Masahiko Tsumura Tsuneo Noda
Role of authors	Masahiko Tsumura - ISO 20000 Consultant Tsuneo Noda - ISO 20000 training course director
Company of authors	Masahiko Tsumura - IP Innovations Inc Tsuneo Noda - IP Innovations Inc
Date of case logging	May 11, 2007

To write this case study, Masahiko Tsumura and Tsuneo Noda interviewed representatives from Nippon Securities Technology Co Ltd in Tokyo, Japan:
- Mr Ryoji Nakamura (Executive Officer, Operation Division)
- Mr Shingo Yagi (Manager, Operation Division)
- Mr Takehisa Makino (Engineer, Operation Division)

6.1   Organization type

Company name	Nippon Securities Technology Co Ltd
Address	Tokyo Dia Building No5 28-23, Shinkawa 1-chome Chuo-ku Tokyo 104-0033 Japan
Type of company	Corporate Limited
Number of Employees (as of March 1st, 2007)	285
Capital	JPY 228 million

Table 6.1   Outline information on Nippon Securities Technology

6.1.1   Main activities

NST offers its clients solutions based on its expert knowledge of the securities business. Specifically, the company is a system integrator, providing coherent services related to securities business systems, from the system planning to the system operation. In addition to this, the company handles the research and development of various systems, and the sales activities of application packages.

As a total solution organization in the securities and financial industry, the company offers full-line IT solution services under the concept of mission critical system development.

Table 6.2 shows the systems and business line focus of the company.

Securities business systems	Business systems for redemption companies
Internet trading systems	Securities home trading system through internet
Investment advisory systems	Financial and institutional analysis system
CRM systems	Database and investment analysis system
Building latest network systems	Building and monitoring large-scale network systems capable of handling multimedia data using internet technology
Other systems	• Financial and administrative accounting systems • Personnel pay system • CIT package sales

Table 6.2   The systems and business line of Nippon Securities Technology

6.1.2   Relevance of IT Service Management

The company aims to provide highly reliable IT services to satisfy their clients' business needs under the concept of 'client first'.

It is important to ensure availability and continuity of IT Service Management through system development to operation and maintenance. To realize this, the improvement of service quality and customer satisfaction is continuously pursued through the implementation of an IT Service Management system.

6.1.3   Customers
The company's main clients are in the financial industry and include:
- Shinko Securities Co Ltd
- Shinko Investment Trust Management Co Ltd
- Mizuho-DL Financial Technology Co Ltd
- DLIBJ Asset Management Co Ltd
- Mizuho-DL Financial Technology Co Ltd

6.2   Drivers for certification
There were three main drivers for obtaining certification:
- Certification offered the company an opportunity to demonstrate to the market its ability to provide customers with highly reliable IT services. The ultimate goal is to be a leading company of IT service within the industry.
- Highly reliable IT services and a high level of customer satisfaction increases the standing of the company as an IT service provider.
- The certification also contributes to the continuity of the business.

> *"First we implemented ITIL as an IT operations standard; however, we found that ISO 20000 works as the yardstick of IT Service Management. Since the scope of the target was quite clear, we decided to work for ISO 20000 certification." Shingo Yagi*

6.2.1   Main initiator
The project was organized as follows:
- ISO 20000 certification project committee: 15 members
- 10 support members from owner sections (divisions such as operation, development and personnel)

For the detailed organization of the project, see Section 6.4.

6.2.2   Business case

2.3.1 Benefits
A benefit of the ISO 20000 certification is that by reporting the current status of the IT service to the service receiver (the customer), it narrows the gap as regards deliverables between the service provider and the service receiver.

Demands for price reduction from the customer are also avoided. The company also demonstrates continuity of service with monthly performance reporting.

Business effects are demonstrated in Table 6.3: Customer Satisfaction Evaluation for Home Trading System (Year 2006).
Evaluation points have increased significantly in terms of the SLA indicator: from 64 to 76%. Total Customer Satisfaction rose to 70% as a result. Customers can rate their satisfaction against either:
- Service Comments
- SLA Index Comments

'Service Comments' consists of 16 questions and ' SLA Index Comments' of five questions. Each question is rated against five levels, from poor (1) to excellent (5). So, if all answers are excellent for 'Service Comments', it gains 80 points (5 points times 16 questions equals 80 points). These points are then converted to a percentage, to give a 100% score. See Table 6.3.

Thus, if 63% is the score for 'Service Comments' in 2005, we could obtain the original score from the following equation:

$$X \; (points \; gained) \; / \; 80 \; (possible \; points) * 100 = 63\%$$
$$X \; (points \; gained) = 50.4$$

Table 6.3 shows the customer satisfaction evaluation result in April 2007.

1. How do you feel for the present IT service you are receiving?				
Questions	2005	2006 (expected)	2006 (actual)	Evaluation
Service Comments (16 questions) in %	63%	–	64%	Fair
SLA Index Comments (5 questions) in %	64%	–	76%	Excellent
Total Customer Satisfaction Points in %	63.5%	70%	70%	Good
2. What do you think about Nippon Securities Technology Co Ltd?				
Questions (36 questions)	2005		2006	
	Plus	Negative	Plus	Negative
Services provided	1	2	2	0
Business attitude of customer service representative	2	0	3	0
Service attitude toward the customer	2	0	6	0
Impression toward customer service representative	2	0	5	0
Impression toward Nippon Securities Technology Co., Ltd.	0	2	1	1
The company's service capability	0	1	2	0
No response	24		16	
Total Points	7	5	19	1
Total Impression Points in %	6		50	

Table 6.3   Customer satisfaction evaluation for Home Trading System (Year 2006)

The survey also shows that recognition of Nippon Securities Technology Co Ltd (as a customer friendly business) has increased from 6% to 50%. In addition to the increased positive response, the response rate itself has also increased.

The questions listed in the second section have several sub-categorized choices. For example, under the question 'Services provided' there are several sets of positive and negative choices. Each choice is counted as one point. Choice sets include:

'Service provided':
- high quality/poor quality
- few mistakes/many mistakes
- quick response/slow response
- reasonable price/fairy high price

Total positive or negative points gained will be 36. The survey shows 7 positive points and 5 negative points out of a possible 36. Total points of 6% result from the following calculation:

- **for the year 2005** - 7 positive points minus 5 negative points divided by 36 possible points times 100 = 5.5
- **for the year 2006** - 19 positive points minus 1 negative point divided by 36 possible points times 100 = 50

Stakeholder interests
Stakeholders have been anticipating the introduction of IT control in the Japanese financial industry for compliance with the Sarbanes Oxley (SOX) Act. Stakeholders think this will help to satisfy the need for IT governance and internal control in its IT service.

Management benefits
An *internal benefit* can be seen with the increased response speed in operations divisions, with co-operation between divisions.

An *external benefit* is the increased customer satisfaction that is achieved by building strong partnerships with the customers.

6.3   Quality management at the start of the project

At the start of the project, the company had procedures and rules to operate IT Service Management, but they did not have either the PDCA cycle to respond to the field issues, or a program for the yearly operating procedure plan.

Before they started implementing ISO 20000, ISO 9001 and ISO 27001 accreditation helped them to provide IT service to customers. Tables 6.4 and 6.5 show the details for these certifications.

ISO 9001 certification	
Initial certification date	December 26, 2003 (Expansion of a Certification Scope)
Certificate number	JQA-QMA10861
Service ranges	Design and Development of Open System and Relevant Software Packages for Finance and Security

Table 6.4   ISO 9001 certification for Nippon Security Technologies

ISO 27001 certification	
Initial certification date	February 4, 2005 (Expansion of a Certification Scope)
Certificate number	01215-2005-AIS-KOB-JIPDEC
Service ranges	The operation Services for Securities and Financial Systems

Table 6.5   ISO 27001 certification for Nippon Security Technologies

Prior to ISO 20000 implementation, NST provided customers with quality IT services by utilizing the measures and policies established by the company's quality improvement committee, and by using their own management tool.

6.4   Parties involved

Staff participated at various stages of the implementation:

- **Management staff** participated at the beginning of the ISO 20000 certification project.
- **Employees** participated at the beginning of the ISO 20000 certification project.
- **Customers** participated at the adjustment stage, to confirm that the SLA and contracts complied with the ISO 20000 standard.
- **Suppliers** participated at the adjustment stage.

Management staff and employees led the project and created draft documents. With regular weekly meetings and through internet mail communication, they promoted the project and created consensus on how to attain the goals.

The project was organized with members selected from each division to support implementing ISO 20000 for the service range of the targeted system. Figure 6.1 shows the project organization.

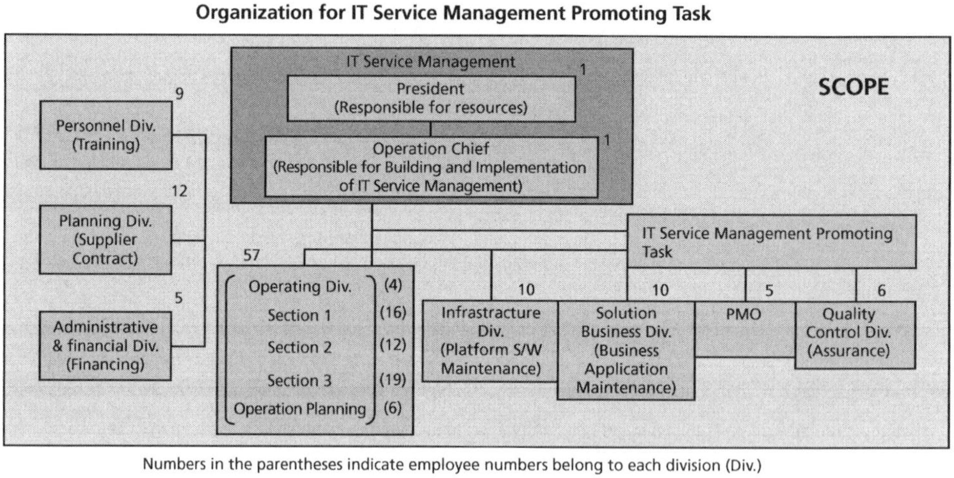

Organization for IT Service Management Promoting Task

Numbers in the parentheses indicate employee numbers belong to each division (Div.)

Figure 6.1   Organization for IT Service Management promoting task

6.5   Initial assessment

Initial assessment based on ITIL, was carried out internally for a period of two months. The assessment checked whether the current status was satisfying all of the requirements within the standard, including the processes, procedures and records.

Prior to the assessment, a current status map was created, based on ISO 20000 and ITIL.

Following the assessment, actions for each of the processes within the standard were identified, and points for improvement were specified. For example, although each division had its task within the organization, the process to achieve the assignment was not clearly specified. Through the assessment activities, the process steps to be taken were well defined.

6.6 Decision to go for certification

6.6.1 Scope

> *"In the scope setting, no serious problems arose, as we set the scope that had previously been determined by an SLA development project which was organized prior to the ISO 20000 certification project." Ryoji Nakamura*

However, a company should determine the scope based on the service agreement rather than on the standard itself, as the relationship between processes reveals inconsistencies, and defined processes tend to differ from the actual processes when they are in operation. However, by synchronizing the index of each process and SLA, inconsistencies between processes were eliminated. In addition, the defining and adapting of the processes was achieved over a relatively short timeframe.

The final scope of the certification was:

> *"The IT Service Management system that supports the provision of the Home Trade System to stock brokerage firms within the technical and organizational boundaries of Nippon Securities Technology Co Ltd in Tokyo."*

6.6.2 Objective

> *"The certification gives us an opportunity to announce to the market that we have the capability to provide customers with highly reliable IT services. This also helps us to achieve our goal to be a leading company of the IT service industry. With highly reliable IT services and customer satisfaction, we are capable of increasing our value as the leading company of IT service providers." Shingo Yagi*

Beside this, the certification greatly contributes to the company by ensuring the continuity of the business.

6.6.3 Funding
Budget was secured for the following items before the project started:
* committee member's man-hours
* consulting expense
* certification audit expense
* expense for ITSM tools

6.6.4 Action and time plan
The project was carried out followed by the ISO 20000 certification plan and the implementation schedule. Figure 6.2 shows the implementation schedule.

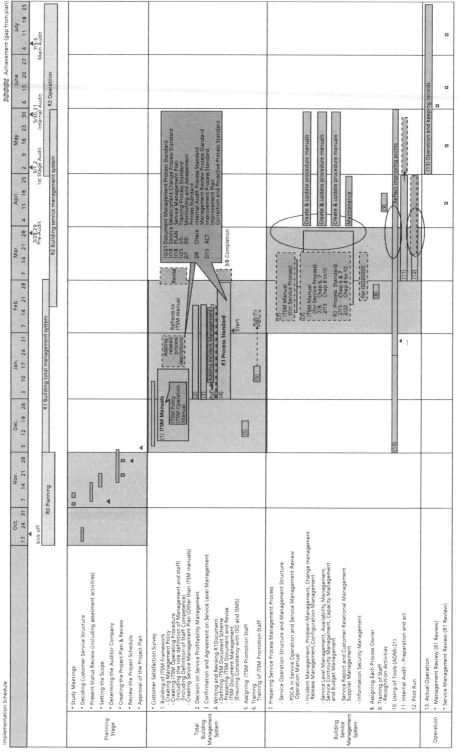

Figure 6.2 ISO 20000 implementation schedule

6.7   Preparation for certification

6.7.1   Selection of the certification agency
The certification agency (DNV certification Ltd) had also been used for the ISMS certification.

6.7.2   Determine scope with certification agency
At the preliminary audit, the scope for the certification was discussed and agreed with the certification agency.

6.7.3   Establish service improvement plan
A service improvement plan was created based on the IT service planning process, to improve the observed gaps. The contents of the service improvement plan comprised:
1. **Overview**
   a. positioning of the document
   b. purpose of the document
2. **Service plan**
   a. ITSM target
   b. objectives
   c. scope
   d. expected effectiveness and service delivery
   e. new and changed service
   f. Service Management activity schedule
   g. precise steps toward the Service Management activities
   h. the organization of the Service Management activities
   i. roles of staff
   j. resources
   k. budget
   l. issue and action
   m. risk assessment and its management
   n. implementation progress review and audit
3. **Project operation**
   a. approval of the project plan
   b. review and revision of the project plan

The director of ITSM management was assigned as the owner of the service improvement plan.

Improvements that have been introduced
In the improvement plan, the following improvement targets were set:
* establish a framework to maintain ISO 20000
* increase of the targeted level of the SLA index
* increased customer satisfaction
* foster project staff (such as internal auditor, promotion staff, implementing staff, etc.)
* keep expense within the budget plus 5%
* ensure adequate capacity
* prepare for suspension of maintenance service (hardware and OS)

Measuring progress

The progress was checked at the weekly project meeting and was measured against the ISO 20000 implementation schedule. A Work Breakdown Structure, specifying process items with person in charge and time schedule, was also used to establish the status of the project.

6.8   Internal audit

It is important to carry out an internal audit, specifying the target of the audit in advance, such as improving customer satisfaction. On-site staff involvement is also essential at all levels. It influences both staff morale and general awareness of project performance.

Previously determined gaps were cleared by confirming that all processes were defined and initiated for the project. Some of the implementation record was found to be insufficient. This was improved and verified by follow-up actions as part of a correction process. A low level of on-site staff awareness was identified in the internal audit at an early stage in the process.

To increase the awareness of the staff for the project, continuous internal announcements and on-site staff training were carried out.

6.9   External audit

The company passed the final audit without any problems and the certification was issued, see Table 6.6.

ISO 20000 certification	
Certification date	July 17, 2006
Certificate number	09556-2006-AQ-LDN-itSMF
Service ranges	The operation services of the Home trade System to stock brokerage firms

Table 6.6   ISO 20000 certification for Nippon Security Technologies

6.9.1   Gaps found

Through the external audit, the following gaps were identified:
- **one minor non conformance** - for agreement on configuration items
- **two observation points** - for specifying process objectives consistent with business objectives and factors for preventive measures

6.9.2   Improvement actions started on these gaps

Although the SLA and agreements should have been added into the configuration management database (CMDB), this was not done, as in the planning phase of the CMDB, the description regarding the operator and the maintenance staff for the CMDB was not clearly specified. This specification was subsequently clarified.

6.9.3   Converting the result into profit

Following accreditation, company sales performance increased (increasing product sales and consultation enquiries) significantly. After the accreditation had been announced to the market the company experienced an increased level of enquiries with regard to outsourcing business.

Certification success was made public via the company homepage and through IT related magazines. It was also announced in the internal company newsletter. A celebration party was held to reward project staff.

6.10   Preserving the certificate

To maintain awareness and also to help retain certification, the company has adopted the following practices:
- service process review (held monthly)
- in-house training (as necessary)
- additional internal audit (twice a year)
- audit training

6.10.1 Metrics and reviews

A KPI (Key Performance Indicator) is defined for each process and used to review the management system to check whether the process meets the indicator. The review result is reported on a monthly basis to the service process review meeting. For example, in the incident management report, the types of incidents which have occurred are analyzed and their categorization is reported.

6.10.2 Interim audits

Service Management activities, internal audit, management review and weekly CAB (Change Advisory Board) including CAB/EC are carried out periodically.

6.11   Evaluation of the business case

"Our ultimate appraisal of the business case is to improve customer satisfaction." Ryoji Nakamura

No adjustments to the costs were needed, as the final cost was as budgeted.

6.12   Project evaluation

Good communication between executives and management is an important factor in running a successful project, in order to avoid critical issues:
- report the objectives and the business needs of the project to executives, and ensure executives' understanding of the project
- ensure executives' understanding of the effective implementation of ITIL's 4Ps (People, Process, Product and Partners) into the project
- the project has to be implemented with on-site staff initiative

Physically independent management databases, such as those for change management, fault management, configuration management and incident management, were used. However, this caused problems as there were no meaningful links between the databases. Given such independent structures, it is difficult to associate items in one database with those in another.

It is important to establish the correct database structure in order to manage the information contained within the different databases successfully.

> *To have a relational database, "we should consider the benefit of the configuration management database and how we should design its mechanism for information management." Ryoji Nakamura*

To solve this, one physically unified database should be built to consolidate each activity, preserving a perfect data relation.

Accreditation led to market recognition in IT Service Management systems. However, further actions are required in the future in order to maintain service quality:

- **Expansion of the scope for the service (now in operation)** - The company is now working to expand the service range to seven customer mission-critical systems, including account systems and its peripheral systems. They estimate that the workload for activity management increases proportionally to the expansion of the service range. They are aiming to trim down the management load by analyzing how activities are categorized into a unified process. It is always necessary to ensure that adequate processes and resources are fully considered in relation to Service Management.
- **Share the concept of ISO 20000 among all employees** - It is important to ensure that all employees fully understand the concept of ISO 20000. It is important to carry out the project by focusing on on-site staff initiative rather than taking the 'top-down' approach. Divisions not dealing directly with customers tend to end up spending more time on management. Improved customer IT service quality cannot be achieved by utilizing the skills of just the operations divisions.

> *"A successful project always requires the support of every section of the company, including the development division and the administrative office." Shingo Yagi*

The following are considered to be important to the successful implementation of ISO 20000:
- **Items not fulfilled in the ISO 20000 implementation plan should be improved:**
  - if inadequate items are identified, suggestions for improvement are provided
  - introduce the PDCA cycle and take a proactive approach, in order to reassure customers that implementation of ISO 20000 works well
  Consider the implementation from a customer perspective
  - straightforward language should be used in the SLA for customers; organize the SLA as a document which is aimed at customers
- **Apply image training for ISO 20000 implementation** - discuss the image of maintenance and management of ISO 20000 among project staff before implementing it, in order to eliminate issues and concerns; it is necessary to determine and get consensus for the direction of the project by image training

"Don't try to explain ISO 20000 to your customers, they are not interested in it." Ryoji Nakamura

6.12.1 Company message

"We think it is important to promote and provide customers with availability and continuity that works together to ensure agreed service levels of IT service, through development to operation and maintenance of our customers' mission critical systems." Shingo Yagi

To realize this, an IT Service Management system has to be implemented in the first instance. Under the system, the company is striving to improve service quality and customer satisfaction.

"By understanding the value and meaning of IT Service Management, the whole company continues to improve and provide better service for the benefit of customers." Shingo Yagi

"It is important to determine and have consensus on the current status of the company, and on the direction that the whole company is heading. Implementation of ISO 20000 has to be undertaken with full understanding of the management system; it is the aim of IT Service Management to bring better service to customers." Takehisa Makino

It is generally thought that ISO 20000 is the standard for IT Service Management to improve the quality of the service.

"We believe ISO 20000 works as a communication tool between customers and service providers to create customer-satisfied IT services." Shingo Yagi

List of acronyms

ACP	Accredited Course Provider
ANSI	American National Standards Institute
AS	Australian Standard
BS	British Standard
BSC	Balanced Scorecard
BSI	British Standard Institution
CAB	Change Advisory Board
CAP	Corrective Action Plan
CEO	Chief Executive Officer
CIO	Chief Information Officer
CI	Configuration Item
CISM	Certified Information Security Manager
CMDB	Configuration Management Database
CMM	Capability Maturity Model
CMMI	Capability Maturity Model Integration
CoBiT®	Control Objectives for IT
CPD	Continual Professional Development
CSI	Continual Service Improvement
CSF	Critical Success Factor
DCURI	Document, Communicate, Use, Review, Improve
EA	European co-operation for Accreditation
EFQM	European Foundation for Quality Management
ENAC	Entidad Nacional de Acreditación (Spain)
ESP	External Service Provider
EUO	End User Organization
FISM	Fellow of the Institute of Service Management
FSC	Forward Schedule of Change
IAF	International Accreditation Forum, Inc.
IRCA	International Register of Certificated Auditors
IS	Information System
ISP	Internal Service Provider
IEC	International Electrotechnical Commission
ISACA	Information Systems Audit and Control Association
ISO	International Organization for Standardization
ISM	Institute of Service Management
ISMS	Information Security Management System
IT	Information Technology
ITIL	Information Technology Infrastructure Library
ITSM	IT Service Management
itSMF	IT Service Management Forum
ITT	Invitation to Tender
JAB	The Japan Accreditation Board For Conformity Assessment
JQA	Japanese Quality Association
KPI	Key Performance Indicator

MI	Management Information
MISM	Member of the Institute of Service Management
MLA	Multilateral Recognition Arrangement
MOF	Microsoft Operations Framework
NAB	National Accreditation Body
OGC	Office of Government Commerce
OLA	Operational Level Agreement
OSS	Operational Support System
PDCA	Plan-Do-Check-Act
PIR	Post Implementation Review
PRINCE2™	Projects In Controlled Environments
QMS	Quality Management System
RAID	Risks, Assumptions, Issues, Dependencies
RCB	Registered Certification Body
RfC	Request for Change
RfP	Request for Proposal
ROI	Return on Investment
RvA	Raad voor Accreditatie (Board for Accreditation, The Netherlands)
SANS Institute	SysAdmin, Audit, Network, Security Institute
SEI	Software Engineering Institute
SIP	Service Improvement Program
SLA	Service Level Agreement
SLM	Service Level Management
SOX	Sarbanes-Oxley Act
SQM	Service Quality Management
TGA	German Association for Accreditation
TQM	Total Quality Management
UC	Underpinning Contract
UKAS	The United Kingdom Accreditation Service

Sources

Sources used in this book

On ISO/IEC 20000

- Bon, J. van (2006). *ISO/IEC 20000, A Pocket Guide.* Zaltbommel: Van Haren Publishing.
- Bon, J. van (Ed.) (2008). *ISO/IEC 20000, An Introduction.* Zaltbommel: Van Haren Publishing.
- Dugmore, J., & S. Lacy (2006). *BIP 0030:2006. Achieving ISO/IEC 20000. Management decisions.* London: BSI.
- Dugmore, J., & S. Lacy (2006). *BIP 0031:2006. Achieving ISO/IEC 20000. Why people matter.* London: BSI.
- Dugmore, J., & S. Lacy (2006). *BIP 0032:2006. Achieving ISO/IEC 20000. Making metrics work.* London: BSI.
- Dugmore, J., & S. Lacy (2006). BIP 0033:2006. *Achieving ISO/IEC 20000. Managing end-to-end service.* London: BSI.
- Dugmore, J., & S. Lacy (2006). *BIP 0034:2006. Achieving ISO/IEC 20000. Finance for service managers.* London: BSI.
- Dugmore, J., & S. Lacy (2006). *BIP 0035:2006. Achieving ISO/IEC 20000. Enabling change.* London: BSI.
- Dugmore, J., & S. Lacy (2006). *BIP 0036:2006. Achieving ISO/IEC 20000. Keeping the service going.* London: BSI.
- Dugmore, J., & S. Lacy (2006). *BIP 0037:2006. Achieving ISO/IEC 20000. Capacity management.* London: BSI.
- Dugmore, J., & S. Lacy (2006). *BIP 0038:2006. Achieving ISO/IEC 20000. Integrated service management.* London: BSI.
- Gartner Inc., 2006. G00136652, ISO/IEC 20000 Has an Important Role in Sourcing Management. Gartner.
- ISO (2006). *ISO 9000 and ISO 14000 – An Introduction.* ISO. Available through: www.iso.org/iso/en/iso9000-14000/index.html
- ISO JTC 1/SC 7 (2005) ISO/IEC 20000-2 – Information technology – Service management – Part 2: Code of practice. ISO.
- ISO JTC 1/SC 7 (2005). ISO/IEC 20000-1 – Information technology – Service management – Part 1: Specification. ISO.
- ISO TC 176/SC 1 (2000). ISO 9000:2000 – Quality management systems - Fundamentals and vocabulary. ISO.
- ISO TC 176/SC 2 (2000). ISO 9001:2000 – Quality Management Systems – Requirements. ISO.
- ISO (2001). *Introduction and Support Package. Guidance on the Documentation Requirements of iso 9001:2000.* Document: ISO/TC 176/SC 2/N525R. Available through: www.iso.org/iso/en/iso9000-14000/explore/transition/2000rev7.html
- itSMF UK (2007). *ISO/IEC 20000 Certification web site.* www.isoiec20000certification.com/index.asp.
- McFarlane, I., & J. Dugmore (2006). *BIP 0015:2006. IT service management. Self assessment workbook. 2nd edition.* London: BSI.

- Page, D. (2006). *Top 10 tips to achieve ISO 20000*. Available through: www.nccmembership. co.uk/pooled/articles/BF_WEBART/view.asp?Q=BF_WEBART_212190
- Read, D (2006). *ISO/IEC 20000. Pitfalls of ISO/IEC 20000 certification programmes*. White paper for PRO-ATTIVO.

On the ISO/IEC 9000 family
- ISO (2006). *Understand the basics*. Available through: www.iso.org/iso/en/iso9000-14000/understand/index_one.html
- ISO (2006). *Explore further.* Available through: www.iso.org/iso/en/iso9000-14000/explore/index_three.html
- Tricker, Ray (2006). *ISO 9001:2000 – The Quality Management Process*. Zaltbommel: Van Haren Publishing.

Other useful sources

On TQM
- Bent, B. J. van der (2006). TQM – *Total Quality Management*. In J. van Bon (ed.) Frameworks for IT Management. Zaltbommel: Van Haren Publishing.
- Bent, B. J. van der (1999). *Organisatieleren: een zoektocht naar de geheugendragers en de rol van organisatiegeheugen in veranderingsprocessen*. Rotterdam: Erasmus University.
- Brassard, M. (Ed.) (1991). *Memory jogger (tools for continual improvement)*. Salem, NH: GOAL/QPC.
- Conti, T. (1993). *Building Total Quality. A guide for management*. London: Chapman and Hall.
- Crosby, P. B. (1979). *Quality is Free*. New York: McGraw-Hill.
- Deming, W. E. (1986). *Out of the Crisis*. Cambridge, MA: MIT Center for Advanced Engineering Study.
- Deming, W. E. (1994, 2nd edition). *The New Economics for Industry, Government, Education*. Cambridge, MA: MIT Center for Advanced Engineering Study.
- Garvin, D. (1988). *Managing Quality. The Strategic and Competitive Edge*. New York: The Free Press.
- Hardjono, T, S. ten Have, & W. ten Have (1997). *The European Way to Excellence*. Brussels: Directorate-Generale III Industry, European Commission.
- Imai, M. (1986). *Kaizen. The key to Japan's competitive success*. New York: Random House Business Division.
- Juran, J. (1988). *Juran on Planning for Quality*. New York: The Free Press.
- MacLeod, A., & L. Baxter (2001). The Contribution of Business Excellence Models in Restoring Failed Improvement Initiatives. *European Management Journal*, Vol. 19, No. 4, 392-403.
- Mulè, G. (2007). EFQM – *European Foundation for Quality Management Excellence Model*. in J. van Bon (ed.) Frameworks for IT Management (second edition). Zaltbommel: Van Haren Publishing.
- March, A. (1996). A Note on Quality: The Views of Deming, Juran, and Crosby. *IEEE Engineering Management Review*, Vol. 24, No. 1, 6-14.
- Martin, P., & Tate, K. (1997). *Project Management Memory jogger*. Salem, NH: GOAL/QPC.
- Nuland, Y. van, G. Broux, L. Crets, W. De Cleyn, J. Legrand, G. Majoor, & G. Vleminckx

(1999). *Excellent: A guide for the implementation of the EFQM-Excellence model.* Leuven: Comatech.
- Peach, R. W., Peach, B., & Ritter, D. S. (2000). *Memory jogger 9000/2000 (implementing ISO 9001).* Salem, NH: GOAL/QPC.
- Ritter, D., & Brassard, M. (1998). *The creative tools memory jogger (creative thinking).* Salem, NH: GOAL/QPC.
- Wentink, T. (1999). *Kwaliteitsmanagement en organisatieontwikkeling.* Den Haag: Lemma.

Websites

• www.isoiec20000certification.com	information on itSMF ISO/IEC 20000 qualifications
• www.iso.org	International Organization for Standardization
• www.bsi-global.com	British Standard Institution
• www.exin-exams.com	information on EXIN ISO/IEC 20000 qualifications
• www.deming.org	Deming Institute
• www.efqm.com	European Foundation for Quality Management
• www.ink.nl	Quality Institute for the Netherlands
• www.juran.com	Juran Institute
• www.kaizen-institute.com	Kaizen Institute
• www.kdi.nl	Dutch Foundation for Quality
• www.olkk.nl	On line kwaliteitskring, Dutch quality circle
• www.vck.be	Flemish Quality Management Centre

Index

P

PAS 99:2006, 45
PDCA cycle, 6, 16
Plan, 13, 55
Policy statement, 13
Problem, 13
Procedure, 13, 25
Process, 25
Process manager, 38
Process owner, 38
Project board, 37, 51
Project manager, 37
Project organization, 37
Project team, 55

Q

Quick improvement opportunities, 71

R

RACI-VS model, 54
Re-certification audits, 9
Record, 13, 25, 27
Registered Certification Body (RCB), 9, 59, 61, 79
Release, 13
Release policy, 24
Report, 49

Request for change (RfC), 13
Resource utilization, 88
Roll-out plan, 24

S

Scope, 28, 41, 44, 46, 55, 61
Scoping statement, 41, 46
Self-assessment, 9
Service desk, 13
Service Level Agreement (SLA), 13, 18
Service Management, 13
Service provider, 13, 32
Service quality management (SQM), 3
Service report, 18
Shalls, 8
Short horizon planning approach, 71
Shoulds, 8
Sign-off, 50
Specification, 7
Stakeholder matrix, 52, 56
Supplier, 31
Support roles, 39
Surveillance audit, 9, 75, 79, 89

T

Trends, 88

Made in the USA
Middletown, DE
11 March 2015